waltzing with the captain:

Remembering

Richard Brautigan

D0770686

by

Greg Keeler

Limberlost Press

Acknowledgments

Thanks to the editors of *Beat Scene* and
Rolling Stock, where excerpts from
this book first appeared.

First Edition

Copyright © 2004 by Greg Keeler

ISBN: 0-931659-93-0
ISBN (Signed Edition) 0-931659-94-9

Limberlost Press
17 Canyon Trail
Boise, Idaho 83716
www.Limberlostpress.com

Cover painting,
back cover photo and chapter illustrations
by Greg Keeler

Greg and Richard, 1982

Table of Contents

Table of Contents

(continued)

Introduction

The stories that follow are my own memories of Richard Brautigan. There's no research involved here. I avoided reading other articles and biographies; while I wrote it, I even avoided talking to friends who knew Richard when I did for fear of getting confused, going off on a tangent, and giving up. No, I pretty much just sat down and plowed through whatever I could conjure up from the various images and fragments of conversation that remained in my head and in old letters he'd sent me. The first third or so, I wrote shortly after Richard's death for a *Rolling Stone* reporter who called and asked for some stories. When he ignored all of them in his article, I gave up writing anything down about Richard for years—except for some poetry and an article I wrote for his friends, Jenny and Ed Dorn and their magazine, *Rolling Stock*. It's included here in the chapter called "Fishing."

Richard once told me that he felt split in two, that there was Richard Brautigan, the famous author, and there was Richard, the guy who lived day to day, the guy sitting in the car next to me who had to deal with the public's responses to the famous author. I think the reporter from *Rolling Stone* was mainly interested in the first Richard, as were reporters from *People, Vanity Fair,* and other magazines that came out with stories about the famous author and his Gothic suicide. After all, that's the job of popular magazines.

I hadn't really planned on publishing this memoir until my friend, David Behr, for a hobby, started a humorous website called "Troutball," where he posted my songs, paintings, cartoons, poetry, and inanities. Since David has long been a Brautigan fan and since he knew I'd been Richard's friend, he asked if I had some stories to post on the site. At first I was a little reticent because I didn't think anyone was interested in Richard, the guy who sat in the car next to me, but David said, "Well, hell, I'm interested," so I typed the old stories into my computer and sent them to him.

After the stories had been on the site a year or so, my friend Rick Ardinger at Limberlost Press, saw them and suggested this book. With that motivation, I sat down, updated the perspective in the first part, and whomped up a bunch more stories. The more I wrote, the more I remembered, and in recreating dialogue, I felt that the Captain was sitting right there next to me again, taunting me about my literary pretensions, making me repeat myself and suggesting that a drink might be in order.

I started calling Richard the Captain after he came back from a reading at Notre Dame wearing a military cap. Lately, I've also heard that some of his friends in other places called him the Captain. To me he was several Captains: Captain Colossal, Captain Belly-Buster, Captain Darkness, Captain Clumsy, Captain Random, Captain Death....

I know that many of his readers and fans are very possessive about their impressions of the author and aren't going to trust comments by a guy who drank with him and drove him around for a few years. I don't blame them. If I were they, I'd probably put more credence in his daughter, Ianthe's book about him—or his long-time friend Keith Abbot's book.

I'm just hoping to give another perspective, and maybe even encourage others who knew Richard to write down their own memories of the man. The more the merrier. Now that I'm through with my own little part, I'm going to start reading what others have to say and try to get a more complete picture of the leviathan that posed as the funny, disturbing, cruel, lovable and, especially, vulnerable man who rode in the car with me.

I have a friend who is attempting to deal with the whole leviathan: William "Gatz" Hjortsberg. Gatz shouldered the official biography many years ago when another friend Tim Cahill, who had originally taken on the project, gazed for a year or so at the enormous chimera looming up before him, shook his head and could well have said something like, "Here Gatz, you do it. I need my life back."

The last I heard, Gatz was still wrestling with the beast.

My thanks go out to Michael Sexson and Chris Schaberg as well as David Behr and Rick and Rosemary Ardinger. Without their encouragement, I probably wouldn't have written this. And without the profound patience of my wife, Judy, and the tolerance of my sons Chris and Max, I probably wouldn't have been able to persist in my friendship with Richard, much less write about it twenty years later.

waltzing with the captain:

Remembering

Richard Brautigan

Four Thousand Dollars

When I first started teaching at Montana State University in 1975, I had heard rumors about Richard's presence in Paradise Valley, around thirty-five miles from Bozeman, but he was just sort of a larger-than-life fog in my mind, blown in from San Francisco where I used to stand stupidly pensive in front of the public library from which I figured he got a lot of ideas like *The Abortion*. It wasn't until I found out where his house was that I actually began to sense a tangible presence. Once I drove by his big blue mail box then ran back and stuck a note in the outside latch asking if he ever might want to come and read in Bozeman. But no response.

In 1977, Gary Snyder came to Bozeman for a week-long residency. While he was here, Marge, the English Department secretary said that Richard had called and wanted Gary to come out and visit him. Before going, Gary told me a little about Richard. He said they were friends, that Richard used to be a Tokay alcoholic when he was a teenager, that he (like Gary) had married a

Japanese woman, and that he (Gary) was going to try to convince
Richard to get more involved with the Montana community (since
Gary was and still is very much interested in community).

When Gary returned, he said that Richard drank a whole lot
of whisky, and at a party, he had passed around a mouse trap and
people took turns sticking their fingers in it and trying to pull
them back before it snapped. Snyder has a way with understate-
ment. It wasn't until about a year later that I got another note
from the secretary. This time, Richard had invited me out to his
place along with two students from the M.S.U. Student Programs
Board. Community involvement moves in mysterious ways.
As I read "bring wine" at the bottom of the note, I didn't know
the magnitude of the tradition that I was to enter. The Captain
wanted a residency at M.S.U.

So there the three of us were, standing on Richard's porch,
holding a bottle of Almaden Chablis and shivering in November
snow. Richard welcomed us in, sporting a torn work shirt, blue
jeans, and cowboy boots. I glanced down at my blue jeans, cowboy
boots and torn work shirt and had a slight premonition. (At one
point in our friendship, I called a stray cat on his place a doppleganger and Richard asked me what that meant.) Akiko, his wife
was beautiful and appropriately inscrutable. As the evening
progressed, the Captain called Flaubert a sack of shit and William
Stafford (one of my favorite people and poets) a cunt (because he

had told Richard that his children enjoyed his books). And after a while, he picked up his long-haired Siamese cat and threw it at my face. I must have responded with appropriate gullible naivete because he calmed down after a while, probably realizing that I didn't fit his preconception of an English prof.

He was very gracious to the students and made them both feel a little embarrassed when they tried to start talking business. "Let's not worry about that stuff yet; you're in the country now. Relax." So we all relaxed and ate some very good spaghetti which he had fixed. Aki let us know that she was interested in finding Japanese friends in Bozeman and maybe even in going to school a little. Late that night, when the students were about to drift off, Richard finally said, "Welp, let's have a ball park figure." The students looked at each other and one of them mumbled "Four...." "Four thousand it is," said Richard. The two students gulped, and that was that. Richard would come in April of '79 for a week-long residency.

When we left, Richard insisted that we take the Trail Creek road home. (We had come via the interstate to Livingston and the two-lane blacktop down Paradise Valley.) Trail Creek is a short-cut that goes up over a dip in the mountains between his house and the Bozeman Pass. Depending on the season, it is gravel, mud, snow, ice, or oiled. Fortunately, the snow hadn't done much and the road was still gravel at that time. Richard and Aki accompanied us to where Trail Creek converged with the two-lane and we bid our first farewell. The Captain liked those back roads. In Paradise Valley, he liked the East River Road which was the old highway on the other side of the Yellowstone River from the newer two-lane. But, as I found out later, the Trail Creek road was Richard's favorite.

The long view of Richard's house and barn from the Trail Creek road.

In the following summers, I would see why as I came up over the pass on that road and saw the bluing Absoroka Mountains with vast foothills, the winding Yellowstone, and in the exact middle of the panorama, Richard's bright red barn. It has now been years since he shot himself, and I still have lots of trouble with my emotions when I drive down into Paradise Valley from Trail Creek.

A week later, my wife, Judy, and I had the two students, Richard and Aki over for dinner. The Captain leaned back in our cheap wicker K-Mart love seat and fell over backwards. As he drank more and more, he started talking in a small Oriental voice and getting very serious. I would later start calling this late night voice the Imperial Mode. At the time, I thought it was a funny voice, a silly pretentious voice. But I was to find that it was a very sad voice.

Aki laid some toothpicks on our coffee table in the shape of a stick-figure dog with a pointed face. Richard said he wanted to find out how our left brains worked, then put a bottle cap behind the dog and called it the moon. "Make the dog look at the moon," said Aki. Richard nodded puckishly. After several embarrassing minutes of feeling like red-socked, hushpuppied, left-brain scientist nerds, we gave up, and Richard tilted the two toothpicks forming the pointed head perpendicular to the table and said "See, now he can see the moon."

Soon the conversation turned to fishing, and Richard said that the winter fishing was coming soon and did I know about the tiny black nymphs that the cutthroat behind his place on the Yellowstone went crazy over when there was slush in the water? I said I didn't but showed him my favorite wet fly. He said, "That's it...with a minor change," and he took some fingernail scissors and cut the hackles off of it. "There you have it," he said imperially.

Later I found out he had caught so many trout with that nymph, he sent Aki trudging through the snow with armloads of fish to give to their neighbors, Gatz and Marian Hjortsberg.

Around midnight, Richard said, "Any more liquor." I had already rustled up odds and ends of Vodka, Gin, and Canadian whisky (after finishing the wine and bourbon). Now everything was all gone. "Time to go," said Richard. Judy wasn't amused, and Akiko didn't seem too thrilled about the exit, but the students were almost asleep and Aki had to drive Richard all the way home over the pass. To my knowledge, Richard never drove.

April Residency

The week-long residency back in '79 is all sort of a blur to me now. I remember a formal evening reading with a small audience. I remember him reading and playing some records of the Japanese pop group, Pink Lady, to a large audience in the music recital hall. I remember going fishing with Richard for the first time. David Schreiber, a novelist student went with us. He was later to become another one of Richard's good friends. We drove out to an irrigation dam on the West Gallatin between Four Corners and Gallatin Gateway. Richard wanted to take some whitefish back to Akiko because she had a wonderful way of fixing them with salt. It was an impromptu trip, so we were waderless with fly rods and a few Woolly Worms. When we got to the first hole, there was another fisherman down the way, and when he saw us, he started darting toward our spot. "Look at his little feeties go," I said. Richard loved that and repeated "little feeties." We beat the fellow to the hole and he walked away with what Richard described as a "crumpled Charlie Brown mouth." After a while, we only had two whitefish and the Captain was nervous because we had to get back for some sort of deadline (his plane I think), and he wanted one more for the recipe to work.

So I dashed off through a deep snow bank, walloped my Woolly Worm out on the water and caught a large stupid whitefish. Richard was pleased and impressed. I later learned that they were a hit at some sort of bash thrown by Francis Ford Coppola.

Tony "Apocalypse" Dingman

I didn't see the Captain again until that summer. His leaving was always mysterious to me, whether he went to San Francisco, Tokyo, Europe or just on tour. Except for Shiina Takako, his Japanese "sister," I didn't know much about the friends he had in other places, and he only brought them up occasionally. He told a couple of wild stories about Dennis Hopper and later, after Richard's divorce, about Don Carpenter, Terry Gardiner ("The Wild Legislator" from Ketchikan, Alaska) and some big guy in California who was going to break Richard's leg if he ever got married again. So when Richard showed up with Tony Dingman one summer evening, I got a pretty clear impression of what kind of people Richard hung out with. "I'd like you to meet Tony," said Richard. "He was an assistant director for *Apocalypse Now.* If you look closely the next time you see the movie, you'll notice his head among several others scattered across Colonel Kurtz's front yard." Tony had had to sit in a pit for several hours so that only his head showed. He said he didn't enjoy that much because there were bugs in the pit, and it was awfully hot—no way to spend an afternoon in the tropics. Tony had been class president in his high school in California, though that was a long time ago. He liked to scrawl wild poems in pencil in a little notebook he carried. I read one called something like "Ode to John Wayne" and though I forget the specifics, I recall that it was wonderfully wild and unpredictable.

Tony, Richard, Aki, Judy, and I spent several evenings eating out, shopping at the Bozeman Safeway, drinking, and driving around town yelling *unko* (which means shit in Japanese) out the car window. I later told this to Snyder and he said Aki must have found it terribly insulting and embarrassing, but she didn't appear to mind. Tony delighted in doing things like getting a running start down an aisle at Safeway and sliding into a potato display yelling, "Look, an Irish manger!" Richard obviously condoned this behavior, but I'm not sure (looking back on it now) that Aki was too crazy about it. After that summer, Tony vanished. I asked Richard about him several times, but he didn't say much—never anything bad—just nothing much. He seldom talked about his friends when they weren't around. Later, I got the impression that Richard had several different lives with types of friends to match them.

Attack of the Thistles

Anyway, that night when Richard and Tony came over for the first time, Tony left as Richard slipped into the Imperial Mode and the booze began to dwindle. David Schreiber came by with half-a-fifth of Canadian and left that with us. Later, Richard asked me to come over and stay at his place that night. Judy said, "Fine, just don't kill yourselves on the road." Over the next few years, she would amaze me with her patience and tolerance, even though it wasn't long before she made sure that the Captain didn't have much to do with her own life. It was late when we got to Pine Creek (the community where he lived on the Yellowstone).

Aki was asleep and so was Tony. That night Richard talked a lot about his land. He had forty acres with a house (a log cabin built shortly after the Civil War and in this century stuccoed over and completely remodeled when Richard moved in), a huge red barn with electric milking machines that still worked, a chicken house (sans chickens by the time I arrived), an outbuilding where a skunk lived behind the barn, a guest cabin (where Richard frequently slept), several abandoned old cars rotting beside the barn (Richard and I spent many an evening lying on the hood up against the windshield of an old Ford Victoria watching the sun set and talking about things that seemed immensely important at the time) and a spring running through the property (later, the source of much unwarranted water-rights anguish). Richard's studio was in the top of the red barn, and we had to walk through lots of pigeon shit to get there for private readings or aimless ramblings.

After describing much of his property, Richard led me out into the yard. Morning was coming up over the Absorokas just east of his house, and, at the time, I felt really honored to be in the confidence of this big, funny, disturbing man. Out in an open place, he pointed south and said "My land goes to the road over there then to the line of trees beyond it." He pointed west to where they were just starting to build a new house and said, "and it goes to where they're starting to develop things over there." He pointed north to a fence and said, "and that's the border between my place and the Hjortsbergs' property." There was no need to point east because the East River Road ran right in front of his house where the property obviously ended.

When he was through pointing in all these directions, he said, "I think the cat's in the bag and the bag's in the river. I think I'm safe. They can't get me now." I was a little surprised about this last part because I didn't know at the time who THEY were and how

Richard's house sat on 40 acres of land.

THEY could possibly GET one of the most famous living writers in America. "But there is one thing," said the Captain with a kind of scary look. "The fucking thistles. They're taking over the whole place." Richard had hired a man to battle the thistles, but that, apparently, wasn't doing the trick, so from dawn until the sun started to get hot, we dashed around his land ripping up thistles, beating their roots against fence posts and stomping them to a pulp until our hands were too torn up to be of use any more. When I got back to Bozeman that afternoon, Judy looked at me and my hands and shook her head.

The Night of the
Living Borscht

ut my first true introduction to Richard's wonderful, scary
craziness came a few weeks after the thistle debacle. He
called me up and said he and Aki were sick of Paradise Valley and
wanted to come to Bozeman for a sort of second honeymoon.
They would get a room at the Holiday Inn and spend a few days
in a "fresh environment." I was delighted that they were coming
and Judy was pretty happy too because I wouldn't be driving crazy
over Trail Creek at all hours of the night. She fixed them dinner
for their first night in Bozeman, and I straightened the house up.
When they arrived, they seemed pretty sullen. Richard was
already in Imperial Mode and was mumbling about borscht.
Akiko helped Judy in the kitchen as the Captain began to divulge
the gruesome details of the previous day.

Apparently, Jimmy Buffet and Jim Harrison were to come to
their house for dinner, and Aki had worked for a day getting
some of her super borscht ready for them. I knew Richard had
high praise for Harrison, though it might have been tempered a

little by jealousy since he had recently sold *Legends of the Fall* to the movies for, supposedly, around a half a million. As it turned out, because of a fishing float-trip on the Yellowstone, Harrison, Buffet and their group had just managed to squeeze the borscht into their agenda before they rushed off to Chico Hot Springs. Because of this, Richard and Aki felt snubbed. Jimmy had walked around the kitchen while the borscht was being served saying, "Hi, I'm Jimmy." This, to me, seemed only natural for a newcomer to the house, but it infuriated Richard, and throughout the rest of the evening Richard would intermittently whisper "Hi, I'm Jimmy," then in disgust, "Popular Culture." All of this dominated the conversation before, during and after our dinner, so no one relaxed very much.

Around eight or nine, Richard said to Aki in his most polite Imperial Mode voice, "Dear, it is time for you to go back to the motel and bathe, powder and prepare your body for me." A "give-me-a-break" look darted across Aki's face, but to avoid a conflict, she did the obedient Japanese wife thing and started out the door. "And don't worry," said Richard, "Greg will bring me to you after we have discussed some things." As soon as she was gone, the Captain's face once more contorted to a sneer, and he muttered, "Popular Culture."

By ten o'clock we were still talking about the same thing. Later, I learned that Richard called this "tracking." He would get on a subject which was bothering him and repeat it over and over again, as if through repetition, he could exorcise the situation—and maybe he could. I know that this type of repetition has its effect in his poetry and fiction, but now I also know that it is fairly typical in alcoholics. After about two hours of drinking and tracking, Richard said, "We must go to Pine Creek and settle some business." I gulped, Judy scowled, and Richard and I trudged purposefully toward the car. I probably shouldn't have gone along with Richard's judgment at times like this, but I could see a strange hole in my normal life opening up and the hole was ominous, interesting, and as strong as a flame to a moth.

Soon we were on our way over Trail Creek, Richard sloshing whisky on the front seat of my Mazda Miser, and I driving as slowly and carefully as the urgency of the situation would allow. As we rattled across the bridge toward the Pine Creek Lodge near Richard's house, he said, "Slow down here. We must make plans. The borscht bandits are in the cabins near the main store. We must Punish them." I started sputtering cowardly drivel like, "But I sort of like Buffet's music," and "I've always wanted to meet Harrison but not like this." The Captain stared at me like he might stare at a maggot in some cheese, and I shut up and obeyed. When we got to the cabins at the lodge, Richard ordered me to drive up into the yard. "Now," he said, "push this cabin with your car. I want it moved." Swept away by the gypsy winds of destiny, I nudged the little station wagon into the yard and lightly bumped the cabin. "Yes," said Richard, "yessss. Now flash your lights and honk your horn." When I hesitated, he reached over and did it for me. We waited for a few seconds that seemed like minutes, but no one came from the cabin.

Then, as if a sudden gust of logic had swept down from the Absorokas, the Captain sat back in his seat, whisky sloshed all over him, and said, "Hmmm, maybe we shouldn't be doing this. There are children in there. Those guys are big and can be pretty mean. They could sue me for all I'm worth. Quick, let's go to my house and hide on the floor." So the next thing I knew, we were on Richard's kitchen floor with all the lights out, discussing the impact of Japanese film on his work–from borscht to "In The Realm of the Senses" in one quick illogical sweep. Then, as he started talking about a Japanese woman picking up an egg with her vagina, a little shock came over his face. "Maybe we should go back to Bozeman now." It was two a.m. "Aki is waiting for me." So back over miles of gravel mountain roads we went, leaving the Buffet/Harrison group in god knows what kind of quandary. I hope they never woke up.

"We must stop here at Denny's," said Richard, as I did my best to get him back over Trail Creek Pass to the Holiday Inn before something awful happened. "I will order her some shrimp. She loves them and they should be a perfect peace offering."

I somehow doubted that. The shrimp order took so long that we ate a hamburger and fries while we waited. Finally the waitress came with a plate of scrawny fried shrimp to go. Richard stood indignantly and said. "You are getting no tip. Your service is so terrible, I just wanted you to know that." I hid my face and darted out in front of Richard, who remained at the door reprimanding the tired, frazzled waitress.

"Good luck," I said as the Captain carried the plate of measly shrimp into the Holiday Inn. I'm not sure if he told me this or if I saw it, but I have a picture in my mind of Richard standing outside of the motel room as Aki bounced the shrimp off of his face and chest, one by one.

The next day Aki and Richard pulled up in front of our house in the White Acre (Richard's huge, old, white hog of a Plymouth). Aki stomped the brakes and Richard's head went slamming into the dashboard. She sat in the car while he came in and explained that she had been doing that all morning.

Rip, Tom, and Tony Torn Meet Their Match at Chico Hot Springs

One summer afternoon (August 20—I should know that date very well) in '81, Richard said to come over, bring Dickel, etc. When I arrived, he told me that we were going to meet Rip Torn out at Chico Hot Springs for drinks later in the evening. That sounded good to me. But what would we do for four hours until then (foolish me). As we stumbled to the car after emptying the Dickel, I was wondering how we could do anything more. When we arrived at Chico, the Torns were waiting: that is, Rip and his sons Tom and Tony. The boys were young, smart, cynical and reminded me a little of Heckle and Jeckle. Rip had apparently insulted the Captain or vise versa years ago, so someone had a debt to settle.

They chose cognac for weapons and took turns with us buying two or three fifths. The amazing thing was that as they drank and the old hackles settled, the boys (mid teens) drank too. We all agreed that Rip was too smart for Hollywood and that he should show them what for. I really liked him in *Heartland* and let him know it. He was appropriately modest and thankful for praise and told me an involved story about the teeth he wore to portray Richard Nixon in a TV drama. Richard, in the meantime, was poking fun at Tom and Tony. After a while one of them dropped to the floor and started heaving. The poor soul crawled out to their station wagon and went to sleep in the back. The other one stuck with it. After the last bottle we were all slobbering happy-sad and making all sorts of promises.

As we drove toward Richard's at about 2:30 a.m., I realized that it was Judy's and my wedding anniversary. I drove over Trail Creek road screaming that night. That's about the last time I drove home drunk from Richard's. I got home and made a feeble apology. I would have done better to keep it to myself. I and the crawling, barfing Torn boy could have done without that night. But, as usual, the Captain called all cheerful the next morning, ice cubes jingling in the background, ready to pay back all the money he had borrowed the night before and wondering if I was coming over in the next day or so.

Years later, *Outside Magazine* asked me to write a review of a collection of angling essays called *Seasons of the Angler.* One of the articles, "The Blunder Brothers," was by Rip Torn, and it culminated in that night at Chico. It accurately described the wild retaliatory drink buying; in fact, it accurately described about everything except for the fact that I ended up buying most of the drinks—or that I was even there for that matter. But in writing this memoir, I've probably left out many people who played an important part in the action. Richard had that effect, to make those around him feel that they were the only ones who counted.

The So the Wind Won't
Blow It All Away Airplane

ichard, Marian Hjortsberg (she and Gatz had gotten divorced), and I spent quite a few afternoons in good weather sitting on her porch or out on the grass drinking wine and commiserating. One such afternoon, shortly before Richard's latest novel, *So the Wind Won't Blow It All Away*, was to come out, he had just gotten a copy of the cover. Richard wasn't too happy with the pink and lavender colors in it, but otherwise, he really liked it. We did too. The picture of the comfy furniture by a body of water really got at what the book is about. After watching the warm sun, mountains, and trees through our glasses of Chablis for a while, the Captain gave me the cover and told me to make a paper plane out of it. I promptly did this, making it as long, sleek and airworthy as possible. I think we all agreed that it looked like a pretty good airplane. Then Richard said, "Get back from the sidewalk about twenty feet and throw it as well as you can. If it goes across the sidewalk, we'll all be rich I tell you, rich! If it doesn't–tragedy." We were all confident that there would be no problem with such a sleek, well-balanced airplane. I stepped back, even waited for a little tail wind, and tossed it. It sailed beautifully to the edge of the sidewalk then took a nose dive. We all looked at the stupid little airplane in horror. It was right at the line of demarcation between failure and success. Richard got down and inspected it very closely and still couldn't decide whether it had made it or not. Even if it had, there was still the question of whether the whole thing had to be across the line or just a molecule or two. I guess then we assumed that the paper airplane was sort of like a football on the goal line where the molecule rule went into effect.

When the book was pretty well ignored upon its publication (even a woman writing for the Captain's beloved *San Francisco Chronicle* raked it over the coals—he said she was a hatchet-person brought in from the outside), I looked back guiltily and wished I had made a good airplane—like most of the others I've ever made.

Richard and My Stuff

I've been writing silly songs about the West since I came to Montana in 1975. Richard really liked them. He had me and our friend "Dobro" Dick Dillof play together at his parties. Dobro's dobro added just the right amount of irony to songs like "I Don't Waltz and She Don't Rock and Roll." After his divorce, Richard even had me sing a more serious song, "Roll on Missouri," over the phone to his girlfriend Masako. I think he was hoping she would see me as an extension of himself. It must have worked because when he stopped seeing her, she continued to write to me. When a Japanese crew came to Richard's place to interview him for a series on FM Tokyo called *Welcome to Hard Times,* he invited me to join him and sing some songs for the show. While I was singing "The Ballad of Billy Montana," a bee stung me and the ensuing drama became part of the recording. FM Tokyo was always interested in Richard. In Richard's words, his work sold "like hotcakes" in Japan. In fact, there were even billboards saying "I read *Trout Fishing in America* wearing my (some Japanese brand) sunglasses," since the Japanese consider it a "dark" novel.

But one time in a sour mood, the Captain had me call them and break off a big contract they were working on to advertise Japanese Jim Beam at Richard's place. Before he called it off, we were thinking of using regulars from the Eagles bar in Bozeman in the ad. One of the reporters hinted that if Richard broke the contract he might commit suicide, and Richard said that was his business but he would never commit suicide himself. He said he wouldn't want to leave a mess for someone to have to clean up.

When the reporters left from recording the segment for *Welcome to Hard Times,* the Captain decided we should try to get me a recording contract. So I recorded some songs on my ghetto blaster out in my garage and Richard sent it to a friend, Paula Bateson (a Korean woman) who worked with Colombia Records. He called her and said it was coming, etc. We figured all of this wouldn't work, but it was basically a what-the-hell-why-not, proposition. Of course, the tape came back quickly with a polite thanks-but-no-thanks response. After that, we decided that playing at parties was enough.

I tried not to ask Richard for any favors. When they came, he volunteered them. I figured that if I asked him to help me, he would gradually grow to resent me like he did so many people who had asked him for favors. He once told me that he had never gotten professionally involved with anyone who he didn't start to distrust.

Another favor he volunteered to do for me involved a screwy little picture of a fish rising into the sky that I painted over and over in watercolors. Richard liked the picture. He also liked how I painted so many copies of the same thing. He liked repetition—in his speech and in his work. Anyway, he wanted to have an exhibit of my fish pictures. He said, "We'll paper a room with 'em, and sell 'em off the wall." I really liked that idea but knew it would never materialize (which it didn't).

Eventually I put the picture on my first chapbook of poems. When I gave him a copy, he called it a "sweet piece of machinery" and sent copies to his friends. He offered to do blurbs for my next book; in fact, my editor sent a galley of it to him as he lay in a dead heap in Bolinas. I felt ironic, stupid, and guilty about that: the first time I'd ever tried to "use" the Captain, he was lying in a festering dead heap.

Richard's studio was in the loft of his barn.

Richard, Masako, and Ianthe

When Richard came back from Boulder, Colorado, with
Masako, none of us could really believe it. His divorce
from Aki had been so horribly painful and Masako was so much
younger than he was–and so much more innocent. She had been
doing graduate work at Hofstra–comparing Yeats' plays and
Japanese noh drama. I think Richard was at his happiest when he
was with either Masako or his Hawaiian Japanese friend Eunice.
One night at my house, he went into a long tracking session about
how he would like to live with both of them at once. (Judy went
to bed and slammed the door.)

It was pretty interesting when Richard's daughter, Ianthe,
came to stay that summer. She is about the same age as Masako, so
there Richard was with his lovely daughter and lovely lover living
there like international sisters. Ianthe seemed very patient with
situations like this and in general tolerant of her father's idiosyncrasies.
A year or so later when the Captain was talking to her fiance on
the phone, he called me over and said, "Here's a big local bruiser.

Tell this guy what you're gonna do to him if he doesn't treat my daughter right," so I got on the phone and gave the poor kid some sort of macho bullshit. He and Ianthe both seemed to be good sports about antics like that.

One night in the wee hours, Richard read "The Love Song of J. Alfred Prufrock" to Ianthe, Masako and me, and his kitchen became an odd little classroom where Professor Brautigan held forth. I was surprised that he liked Eliot so much since, in general, he seemed to avoid academic poetry. Richard also liked Robert Lowell's *Notebooks;* he didn't like Sylvia Plath's work, not so much because of the content as the fact that she killed herself with her children in the house.

A Party

I had Richard to several parties at my house and attended several at his. The first party I attended at Richard's was a lesson in psychodrama. Tony was still there, back in the Aki days of 1979. It must have been in the winter because I remember snow. A bunch of Aki's relatives were there with children. I was still fascinated with the newness of knowing Richard, and Judy was already a bit disgusted. The Captain held me on his lap in the kitchen—I weighed well over 200 pounds—and bounced me like a baby. Richard went into Imperial Mode at around ten, and, for some reason, started getting mad at Aki's relatives.

I think he was on some experimental medication for his herpes. Anyway, he went out to the barn with David Schreiber and started smashing a ping pong table they had set up into splinters then stomping on the paddles and balls. Later he came into the house and got a .45 and was threatening to shoot a hole in the floor. When Aki tried to stop him by saying, "Richard, there are children sleeping upstairs," he said flatly, "It's my floor and I'll shoot it if I want to." Finally, he was talked out of it, the kids could sleep in peace, and Schreiber sneaked all of the ammunition out of the house. Not a shot was fired in the house (though as usual there was plenty of shooting of many different weapons off of the back porch at things such as a television, a Japanese pinball machine, a bath tub, etc.)

Sometimes Richard DID shoot his guns in the house. Once he told me that Dobro Dick and a friend had come in with an accordion (the ol' squeeze box) and Richard had a large caliber rifle in his lap. Just to torture Dobro—which he loved to do—he fired it at an angle into the floor. Also once Brad Donovan and Richard took a very nice dining room chair left over from the Aki marriage and filled it full of bullet holes. I had it in my garage for years calling it Montana State University's Brautigan Chair. But it eventually fell into too many pieces.

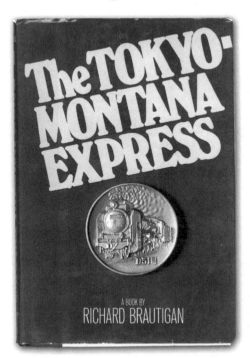

That evening the party ended peacefully with Richard reading me his "Carp Taxi" episode from *Tokyo Montana Express* out in his studio.

Dobro Dick

When I was at Richard's wake (at Marian's), *People Magazine* called and wanted to talk to some of us about Richard. I had gone over to the Captain's house with Sean Cassidy, another of his friends, so I missed out on the fuss. We were wandering Richard's path between his house and his barn studio. The path still really seemed fresh, even though there was some early snow on the ground. We talked about suicide. When we got back to Marian's, Dobro Dick Dillof said that he had talked for half an hour to *People* and tried to do the best he could. Later they called again when Tom McGuane was there. Most of what they used in the article was from Tom. None was from Dobro. That was too bad because Dobro was Richard's favorite object of ridicule. Dobro is a mysterious old-style musician, cowboy drifter. Then, he lived in a sheep wagon behind Marian's place and lured young women from Livingston back there to listen to his weird, quaint instruments and to surrender to his wiles. Dobro plays every song and instrument from sea chanties on the squeeze box, to ditties on some weird middle-eastern sounding bow-played instrument. Dobro was the Captain's fool when I wasn't.

When Dick was hustling a woman in a bar, Richard would sneak up behind him and say "Let's hear a little ditty on the ol' squeeze box." Once Richard actually followed him and his latest girlfriend to Dick's room at the Murray Hotel in Livingston. While Dobro tried to impress the woman with ditties on the ol' squeeze box, Richard stripped completely naked on the bed and lay making alluring gestures at Dobro. Dobro said he wound up getting the best of Richard that night, but from the way Richard described it, that seems impossible.

Sometimes when I came over to pick up Richard and drive him back to Bozeman (usually to drink at the Eagles Bar), Dobro would be standing in front of Marian's in the slanting snow holding an instrument case and waiting for a ride. Richard would point ahead and say, "Drive on," and we would leave him standing there in the snow.

Occasionally, the Byzantine vendettas between Richard and Dobro got a little out of hand. It was like dueling coyotes. When Dobro got wind that the Captain didn't appreciate his comings and goings to the sheep wagon behind Marian's (and also obliquely behind Richard's), he set up his toilet right against the fence between the two properties, as if to mark his territory coyote-style. Perhaps because of Dobro's cowboy hat and his Western ways, the

Captain frequently liked to use guns to make points with him, so it wasn't long before he had the ol' 30.06 out, blasting away at the target-sized white ring of the upraised toilet seat.

Dobro was also a close friend of Jenny and Ed Dorn at the University of Colorado. When Richard went to Boulder for a residency, he spent much of his time with the Dorns and Dobro. Jenny got a little tired of Richard's constant taunting of Dick, but Ed, I think, convinced her that it was always affectionate. When Richard died, Ed, Jenny, and Dobro all felt like they'd lost a true brother. The Dorns invited me and Dick down to Boulder to perform at a memorial, and I got to know Jenny and Ed as a sort of an extension of Richard's memory.

Not too long after the suicide, Dobro told a strange story about how he awoke to find the skin on one of his favorite banjos punctured with a score of tiny holes about the size of a nail file tip. Instead of getting too upset about it, he took it as evidence of Richard's persistent postmortem taunting.

Richard's friend Eunice Kittigawa fishing on Maui.

Professor Brautigan

I first saw Richard teach a class first hand when he took over my evening class in Contemporary Poetry in the spring of 1981. He was good. The acting head of our department, Duayne Hoynes, sat in on the class too (and loved it, even though he was a dyed-in-the-wool Reagan Republican). Richard listed several minutes worth of influences on his work, talked about how he saw various movements in American writing and scanned the class for attractive women. The class hung on every word. I never came close to holding their attention like that.

That next winter he was living in Hawaii with his friend Eunice Kittigawa, a very kind Japanese-American woman who loved Richard so much she would call me sometimes when he was out of the country trying to find and comfort him. I always did my best to relay his address and forward the tee shirts she sent on to Richard. One night he called at about one a.m. from her house in Hawaii and asked if there were any possibility of his teaching at Montana State that spring. Since we had a young, brand new, optimistic, Italian-American department head, I figured that his chances were better than average. After several more late-night strategy sessions, Richard finally called the department head, Paul Ferlazzo. Paul liked Richard's work and was really enthusiastic about getting him here, so at 2:00 a.m. one winter night in Bozeman, the wheels started turning.

Thanks to a sympathetic academic vice president, Stuart Knapp (we called him the dharma dean), Richard was at work here in the spring of 1982. The Captain's students were picked from English majors by English faculty, which might not have been fair, but because of time and number limitations, it was expeditious. I picked a student who had been good but a problem for me. In my own creative writing class, this student had done the following for his class project: He came into the room, put bags over all the students' heads, handcuffed a dictionary to me and put a beer in my hand. He then went to the podium and proceeded to mock my teaching style. In spite of this, I thought his poetry was somewhat like Richard's and he was very bright.

As Richard's class got into swing, he would sometimes ask me to read over the students' papers. Once he said, "Read this," and handed me a paper by the student I had chosen. It was a wild, self-indulgent, semi-surreal poem, and I recognized the style immediately. "Not bad," I said. "Not bad," said Richard with awe on his face. "This fucking stinks. This is a fucking pile of pig shit. Who put this asshole in my class?" "Er, I guess it was me," I said, preparing to be the immediate subject of a long tracking session. "You think this is good?" he said, waving the paper in my face. As it turned out, the student's first comments in Richard's class had been something like, "I don't like your work," and "You call this teaching." But over all, Richard's class liked him and he liked them. He did play favorites, but that was based on whether he liked their work or not. At the end of the quarter, he invited his favorites out to his ranch for dinner.

There was also a girl in the class who started it out with "I don't like your work." Richard went to Paul Ferlazzo for help with her since he didn't want to mess things up. Paul gave him some really good advice, the girl wound up liking the class a lot, and Richard admired Ferlazzo from then on. When Richard departed Bozeman for the last time, he left a whole set of her papers with his comments on them with me since, somehow, she had graduated from the class without them. So, Susy Roesgen, if you're out there somewhere, I have your stories with Richard's comments on them. In fact, here are some of Richard comments.

> Dear Susy,
> this poem has an interesting movement to it.
>   R.B.
>   Sunday Breakfast in November
>
> Jump up from the crystal table,
> flee Momma and her muffins and tea,
>   the door and start breathing --

Dear Lucy,
I'm glad that you wrote
this very honest piece
of writing

WORDS FROM A WALLFLOWER
(OR: An Evening at the Molly Brown

Sometimes I go to a bar to listen to the band. I
of friends who dress to kill, but who are themselves pu
hunted and captured, willing prey for the men who wait
with easy smiles and secret wants.
"It's urgent/ so urgent/ that's why you call me
night."
I have one friend who's convinced th

I wish you luck finding a plot.
I've had the same problem.
RB

She would never be beautiful. She was attractive, s
that, but she was not beautiful. She saw the way some o
older boys in school looked at her, and knew that Mr. Ki
at her from behind the register at Kings 7-11 whenever s
in to pick a carton of milk for her mother.
But she knew she would never be beautiful. She
because she had a subscription to Sevent
month.

One thing that I thought was particularly poignant to come out of Richard's reactions to the teaching experience was his horror at finding out that students actually evaluate the teachers at the end of the quarter. He couldn't believe it. He tried to imagine Zen students grading their masters. "When did this happen?" he said, as if referring to a World War that he hadn't heard about before. I said it was sometime between when I stopped being a student and started being a teacher. As it turned out, Paul was perfectly willing to let Richard skip class evaluations since, for him, it was a one shot deal.

Outside of class, Richard and I managed to keep our lives as unacademic as possible. As usual, we hatched great goofy plans which never came to fruition. My favorite was his idea of buying a large bucket of Colonel Sanders chicken and wandering around among sun-bathing coeds on campus until we found a true winner. Then we would award her the bucket of chicken and she would fall madly in love with Richard.

We usually went to the Eagles Bar before Richard's class for lunch but no booze. That always came after class. Once when I was up ordering Richard's and my burgers at the bar, a local artist shouted from his table something like, "Hey, star sucker, do you always wait on him like that." That artist always had a way of insulting me in public, so I was accustomed to it, but it made Richard furious. "Who does that fucker think he is?" So when our orders were ready, Richard went up, got them, and brought me my burger on his knees, saying, "Lawzy Massah, here be you boiger."

Lady Marian

Shortly after I had become friends with Richard, Gatz and
Marian Hjortsberg got divorced. They are both good people,
so seeing them and their kids get hurt wasn't pleasant. But after
Gatz left, Marian stayed in the big old Victorian house next to
Richard's place with her son Max (also my younger son's name)
and her daughter, Lorca. Though she had (has) a close friend in
Becky Fonda and her sister Ros, she probably saw more of
Richard than most other people around her—when he was staying
at his house. Richard and I went to Marian's just about every time
I visited him and she was home. I like to smoke trout behind my
house in an old refrigerator (which the Captain gloomily called
Auschwitz), so I would bring Marian smoked fish whenever I
had extras.

I remember one wild evening when Richard, Marian, and I
went to a party put on at ex-governor Tom Judge's place. There
were a lot of wealthy people there from up and down Paradise
Valley and Richard was getting pretty feisty with them. If there's

one stereotype Richard disliked, it was that of the yuppie. He had watched them destroy San Francisco by driving people out of their homes and converting them to town houses. He sneered and mumbled as we ate BBQ beef and beans then wandered around the heavily stocked trout ponds. As we left, he said, "Well, at least I've made MY mark," obviously put off by the brandishing of wealth at the party.

When we got to the Emigrant Bar on the main highway, the three of us went in, and there was one of the wealthiest, most ego-tistical people we had seen at the party. He sat at our table, pretty obviously flaunting his acquaintance with Richard. Several cosmic cowboys were at the bar behind us when the Captain decided to change the tone of things, took out his Buck pocket knife, opened it, and started stabbing away at our table. He then dropped the knife in Mr. Upwardly Mobile's whisky. The whole bar took a big breath, and I wished that I was back in Richard's kitchen eating beany weenies. But Marian saved the day. She daintily plucked the knife from the whisky glass, licked the blade, folded it up and put the knife down. The general breath was exhaled, unheard applause went around the bar, and things calmed down. But Marian must have contracted some kind of psychological venom from that blade because before the evening was over, she stumbled outside and passed out in a ditch where we had to find her before we could take her home.

Judy and Richard

I mentioned earlier that my wife, Judy, set herself apart from Richard right at the beginning. After he asked her to fix dinners a couple of times and didn't show up for them, and after he stayed at our house for the first few days of his quarter-long residency, Judy knew that she wasn't going to be nearly as cooperative as I was in taking care of the big goof.

One day while he was staying with us, he walked into the living room with a towel around him, fresh from the bath and asked, "Where should I put these dirty clothes." Judy said "Up in the washing machines at faculty housing" (where the university had reserved a place for Richard). Right after that, he moved up on campus. Other times when he would start tracking in our living room into the wee hours, Judy would go in the bedroom, slam the door, and put a pillow over her head. She got really upset with me when I would let Richard use me for rides, booze money, a social straight man, etc. I would get upset too, but not enough to put an end to it.

Richard ultimately got so apprehensive about Judy that when we came to our house, he would sit out in the car so he didn't have a confrontation. Really, the thing that caused this was when he overheard Judy tell me, "Richard makes me nervous." He tracked on that as he sat in the car and I went in to get smoked fish, whisky, money or whatever.

The Captain made me nervous too, but somehow I felt that his friendship was worth all that. I remember when he came for the quarter residency, he was so nervous himself about confronting a class of students that he followed me around wherever I went: out to empty the trash, out to buy gas, grocery shopping, etc. He reminded me of Harvey, the big invisible bunny in that play.

Montana Elephant Spring

In the spring of '82 while Richard was teaching at Montana State, the two of us came up with perhaps one of the stupidest spectacles of all times: Montana Elephant Spring. It all started when the Captain and I would bar-hop through the wet snow at night. He was trying to impress a barmaid at a place called the Snow Shoe Bar. He had already confiscated my only copy (signed) of *Willard and His Bowling Trophies* and signed it over to her. She had never heard of it before but thought the cover was "kinda cute." When that didn't work, we used the ol' Elephant Man attention getter.

I had a hat (sheep herder's) that I got when I was in the Peace Corps in Turkey. If I pulled it all the way down over my head, I looked a little like the Elephant Man. The effect was complete when Richard paraded me around bars like my trainer, and I slobbered through my hat, "I'm not an animal. I'm an English Professor." But this also had little or no effect on the oblivious barmaid. However, a couple of days later, the image returned to

Richard, and he came up with a plan. "Let's put on a play at the Eagles," he said. As usual, I was game.

And here is the plan as it ultimately evolved. We were to somehow get a half dozen barrel-shaped 50s-style vacuum cleaners with long hoses; a metal wash tub full of mud; our friend Brad; Brad's wife, Georgia; Georgia's sister, Mary; and a plumbing plunger. We were then to take all of these people and this equipment and put it on the stage of the Eagles Bar. I was to get in front of a microphone in typical Elephant Man posture and slobber my professional woes out to the audience while the Captain worked the plunger in the tub of mud and the Donovans shouted words of encouragement. And of course, all of the vacuum cleaners would be running and spread out symmetrically before us.

But, as usual, the plan died down when Judy, upon hearing of it, confronted Richard with, "and what do you think the cowboys and old farts in the Eagles are going to do to you if you go through with this?"

The Eagles Bar

During happy hour at the Eagles, you could get two shots of George Dickel for one dollar. David Schreiber was the bartender there and he always made sure that there was plenty of Dickel. This in itself made the Eagles into nirvana for the Captain. But even as cheap as the primo booze was and as liberal as Schreiber was with the shots, Richard sometimes worked up tabs over $200 in a night buying drinks for himself and friends.

Burger night on Friday was the extra special time, though Richard was at the Eagles many other nights too. On burger night, he held court. Brad and Georgia Donovan, Dobro, Scoop (Karen Datko from *The Bozeman Chronicle*), Sean Cassidy, Mary (Georgia's sister), and friends and admirers from the town and the university would cluster at Richard's table, and he would entertain the troops by doing things like hiding a turkey gizzard in a tumbler of ginger ale and trying to trick Dobro into drinking it or having me slobber through my hat or having Mary strut across the room so he could leer at her.

David Schreiber at the Eagles Bar.

Even the old established Eagles Club members and the alcoholic regulars grew to know and like Richard. Many of them would bring him samples of their writing and talk for hours about literature with him, and he would be more kind, patient and understanding than a paid professor. The Eagles Club members even offered Richard the honor of joining their organization. He was no hotshot outsider; he became the insider. As worn and fruit fly infested as that bar seemed, there is still something magic about it, though, to me, it is like a giant empty tomb now. When Sean Cassidy and I heard about Richard's death, we went down to the Eagles, bought black Eagles hats for mourning and set up a glass of Dickel for Richard.

Ironically, it was the last bottle they had, left over from when Richard went away a year before. We finished it off but left the Captain's glass full on the table. I wasn't so sure it was such a good idea, but Sean took me around to all of Richard's old haunts to start making it bearable. Bozeman Creek runs right under the Eagles bar, and in the spring when the water is high, during rare silence at Richard's old table, you hear it.

Hamburgers

Today we are eating
our hamburgers for
Richard. We don't
know what else to do.
Today we are holding
our hamburgers like
pools on the Gallatin
hold leaves.

Today, in the Eagles
Bar, Montana has made
winter out of October:
out there, wet snow.
In here, the fruit
fly on the edge
of the whisky glass
we've set up for him
doesn't know where
else to go.

As tiny as it is,
we still have no
problem seeing that
its eyes are red.

Today our hamburgers
taste like Bozeman
Creek sounds, running
low beneath us, then
under Main Street,
the Bozman Hotel,
the open sky.

Today, at his ranch,
the kitchen clock is still
full of bullet holes.

Today, we do not
let our hamburgers slip.
We decided that they
should be double-burgers,
loaded. When we ordered
we said, "Give us
double-burgers, loaded."

And now, we are almost
finished. There are
two miracles:
1. Nothing has fallen
to our plates.
2. His glass is full.

A Lesson in
Conceptual Criticism

In the late fall of '82, I had made friends with a Scot named Roger Millar who had come to M.S.U. as a one-year replacement for a sculptor in the art department. Roger thought Americans were fat, decadent and overpaid; he was also a big fan of Richard's work in Scotland, so I decided to treat him to an afternoon with the Captain. Before we left Bozeman, it was snowing pretty hard, but we bought a bucket of chicken for the Captain's dinner and headed over Bozeman Pass on the interstate. When we arrived, Richard was a little stir crazy from being alone at his place, so he was in fine form. He flipped into a brief session of Imperial Mode and told Roger that his house was built on an ancient glacial moraine. He then brought out a baby's bracelet made out of small white beads with a name spelled out on them.

"I found this when they were remodeling the bathroom," said Richard. "It belonged to the baby of the original owner of the house."

Instead of showing the usual star-struck awe in the presence of a great writer waxing eloquent, Roger said, "Bullshit, the fuckin' thing's made out of plastic," (and I think it was). "And this isn't a fuckin' moraine either," said Roger "It's just a little stream bed."

Richard's eyes got kind of funny, like there were a lot of little dots in front of them. He looked at me and said, "My, he's a feisty little fucker, isn't he?" Roger picked up the gauntlet and ridiculed Richard on every stupid point, and the Captain loved it—so much that he gave him signed copies of several of his rare books. I drooled as he lovingly signed away a hardbound copy of *Revenge of the Lawn.* Soon Richard had the mouse trap out and was daring us to try to spring it without getting snapped. Roger said, "You fuckin' gotta be kidding." I stuck my finger in boldly and got it badly snapped. Richard stuck his in and got his badly snapped too. Roger tapped his foot and shook his head at both of us. "That's all you Americans are interested in, violence."

"Ah," said the Captain, "yes, violence," and he darted to the utility room and came back with a .357 magnum. Roger suddenly stopped looking so feisty. He was getting a solid glimpse of American horror. "What shall we shoot," said Richard, looking intently at Roger. "How about that book of criticism you showed me yesterday," I said. "Splendid," said Richard. "Actually, I have two copies of it. That way the hole will be a lot bigger when the bullet comes out through the second one." The book is called *In the Singer's Temple,* and it is by an author named Jack Hicks. The part that made the book quite shootable in the Captain's eyes reads like this:

*"It has become a popular critical pastime to dismiss
Richard Brautigan's writing as merely faddish, a more hip,
barely weightier version of Rod McKuen's maunderings.
Brautigan's poetry does little to discourage this sort of over-
reaction. It seems so uniformly slight; arch, almost unbearably
naive, it is consciously unself-conscious (picture a moronic
adolescent friend waving hello from a televised bowling show)."*

"You shoot them," said the Captain. "I wouldn't stoop to paying
that much attention to this crap." So, as Roger watched in terror, I
took the books out, lined them up and shot them right in the middle.

"Wonderful," said Richard. "Talk about post-modernism."
He picked one up and pried it open. "When you open these babies
up, there's a little round book that opens up and reads by itself
where the bullet went through." Richard was right. We took turns
flipping through the little round book in the middle of the second
book. One internal page read, "it in a black printed nicely the cover."

"Conceptual criticism!" said Richard. And even Roger had to
agree. It WAS conceptual criticism. After that, the Captain and
Roger drank a pint of pure grain alcohol that had been sitting
around Richard's kitchen for a few years; then, they went out on
the back porch and had a good simultaneous vomit or "bok" as
Roger called it in his Scot's dialect.

Richard used Jack Hicks' In the Singer's Temple for a lesson in conceptual criticism.

That night, I was stone sober as I drove Roger back over the pass, hanging his head out the window in the blowing snow and streaking the side of my Mazda Miser.

Later, I heard that Richard had signed the front copy of the book (the one with the smaller hole) over to Peter Fonda, but I still have the second one with the little book in it.

About ten years after this conceptual criticism when I was at U. Cal. Davis performing and giving a workshop with Gary Snyder, I met Jack Hicks, the author of *In the Singer's Temple*. He was a nice guy. I didn't mention that I was familiar with his work.

Sex, Drugs and Rock & Roll

For the bard of the flower children, Richard didn't exactly fit the stereotype of a hippy. As for music, the themes from spaghetti westerns or the Japanese pop group Pink Lady were about the wildest sounds I ever heard coming from the dusty old turntable in his living room. I have several images of Richard lurching around looking for documentation for his income tax forms, worrying about water rights or waiting for a guest, all with the whistling, jingling and pum pumming of *A Fist Full of Dollars* playing in the background. And I have a vague feeling Richard hadn't even bought those records but that they were left over from the Aki days.

Sometimes we'd drive into Livingston and go to a bar where rock, country or swing was playing, but while couples madly two-stepped and jitterbugged in front of us, we'd just stand there like a couple of aliens watching rocks erode. Richard might get interested if a pretty woman were singing with the band or doing a particularly lurid dance, but for the most part he stood there like a big effigy of mud.

65

As for drugs, alcohol was Richard's depressant of choice. If anyone dared to bring out a joint in his presence, a dialogue like the following was bound to ensue:

"Ah, I see you are planning to 'turn on'."

"Er, yeah—want a hit?"

"I assume that you realize you're indulging in an illegal activity."

"Ya think?"

"Perhaps you may not view the subject as being so humorous from behind bars with a baby face and an asshole three inches wide. Perhaps if you want to break the law you should do it out of my presence so that the legal system won't include me in your act of hooliganism."

"Well, what the hell then, let's go get us a big fawkin' drink."

"Now you're speaking my language, big fella. Not only is alcohol legal, but it's very predictable. You always know where it's coming from, and, for the most part, you always know where it will take you."

And maybe it was true. Maybe Richard did know where alcohol would take him, even, perhaps to that eventual rendezvous with a .44 magnum sandwich, but when I would follow him on the trail of that jingling golden-brown beast, I sure as hell had no idea where we were going. Here's sort of an amalgam of our bar-hopping sorties:

We walk into the Livingston Bar and Grille after several drinks at the Hyatt House, The Guest House, and The

Yellowstone Inn. I see a friend, Tandy Riddle, who says,

"Hi Greg, how are your classes going over at the U."

"Shut up, asshole," says Richard. "I'm here with my friend to have a few drinks, and no one asked for you to butt in."

"Jesus," says Tandy, "Can't I say hi to a friend."

"MY friend doesn't talk to ASSHOLES. MY friend is here to talk to ME."

"It's O.K.," I say. "I know Tandy from way back." (Oddly enough, when Richard met Tandy at a more sober moment, they became good friends, and she still speaks fondly of the compassion and humor that lurked under Richard's abrasiveness.)

Then I apologize to Tandy and I steer Richard over to the bar where we sit on stools and he promptly reaches around and taps the cowboy on the other side of me on the shoulder.

"Hey, partner, my buddy here wants to fight you."

"Huh–wha...," says the cowboy.

"You heard me, pard."

"He's drunk," I say. "He doesn't mean it," I say.

"God," says the cowboy, "That's all I need–more dental bills."

"Tell me about it," I say.

"I think these two love birds need a drink," says Richard.

"What's your poison," says the bartender.

etc.

Or perhaps we'll be sitting in the Eagles Bar in Bozeman and a dance will be in progress upstairs—say the annual ball for older Eagles members and their wives. While the bottle of Dickel gets lighter and lighter, the sixty to ninety-year-old women get more and more attractive to us as they wander up and down the stairs to take a breather or get a drink in their sparkling colorful gowns and dresses.

"Look at the one in green," says Richard. "I'll bet, in her day, her daddy had to drive 'em away with a ten gauge.

"But hey," I say, "she's nothing compared to that one at the bar with a Grasshopper. I mean she's in pretty damned good shape the way she is."

An hour passes.

"Sweet bleeding Jesus, I gotta talk to that one. I think I'm in love. I think I can take her husband, if he'd lose the cane."

"Hold it there buster, I saw her first."

Then in a moment of crystal clarity, through the smoke, alcohol, and buzzing fruit flies, Richard says, "Hey, why don't we just skip all the banter, go into the Ladies' Room and hang our tongues over the toilet paper roller."

Because sex, along with alcohol, probably destroyed Richard in the end, it's only logical that, in his more lucid moments he should make it the subject of his darkest laments and sharpest humor. He frequently made fun of his own sexuality with comments like, "I sure would like to give HER a good time. If I only had a couple

of rubber bands and a Popsicle stick for a splint!" Or "There were
two lovely women at my Notre Dame reading who were ready to
go. If it weren't for these damned herpes we could have done a
tricycle!" After Richard died, I heard wild sordid stories about how
he liked to tie willing women up. His fiction dwells on this too, but
he never discussed it with me–and neither did his women friends.

Once in the Baxter (Robin) Bar in Bozeman, he took a spoon,
put its convexed side down where he'd penned in a black spot
between his index and middle finger, gyrated his hand so that the
reflection in the spoon looked obscene and said, "Look, a North
Dakota skin flick!"

Sometimes, to relieve the boredom of an afternoon, Richard
would recount odd sexual exploits. I was never sure if he was
making them up or not, but, because the stories were so quirky,
I ultimately believed them. One of the oddest involved a woman
I knew who was a local actress. In an effort to help her career,
Richard had invited several people from the university theater arts
department over to his house for dinner. Before they arrived he
asked the woman to put a remote controlled sexual device in
herself (to which she happily obliged), and during key moments
throughout the dinner and following drinks and conversation,
he would activate the device.

In another story, he told me how he once had rather noisy anal
sex with a woman and tape recorded the whole episode. Afterward,

while she bathed, he put the tape recorder next to the tub so that she could listen to what had just transpired, and she became so aroused that she got out of the tub and they continued where they had left off.

Shortly before Richard's suicide in 1984 when I visited him in Bolinas, he said that he had been hitchhiking on the local highways, hoping that someone would pick him up as "road meat."

In the time that I knew him, even though it was just before the AIDS epidemic took hold, Richard was very careful about having sex (when he could have it) because of his herpes. His own case horrified him, and he would go to extremes to keep from spreading it. He told me sad stories about a Japanese woman he knew who had herpes so bad she had to crawl around her apartment because she couldn't walk.

Once while he was teaching, he wrote a sample story for his class about an alien race of sores on another planet who had to trudge to a dark gloomy place called The Grotto to be drained. Little did the class know that Richard was writing about his own raging herpes and that he had just been in a tiny park on campus called The Grotto where he had been sitting on a little bench in front of a sun dial examining his herpes.

Sometimes his outbreaks would get so bad that he would go to extremes. One Sunday when I was away at an academic conference, he dared to come to our house to beg the dreaded JUDY for a little corn starch since all the stores that sold talcum powder in the vicinity were closed.

Another time he sat Georgia Donovan's young sister, Mary, down at a table at the Eagles and gave her a long lecture on herpes.

"Never, ever have sex with a man unless you examine him first," said the Captain.

"Eeeww," said Mary.

"No, I mean it," said Richard. "Get right down on your hands and knees and have a good close look at it. If you see so much as a red spot or a bump, drop the guy like a hot potato. It's not worth it."

Occasionally, the Captain caused me to wonder a bit about his own sexual preferences, but I imagine this was to make me ill at ease, a state which he took great pains to nurture in me. For example, once in the Eagles Bar on Friday burger night when the place was full of blue-collar rowdies, ranchers, and carousing art students, Richard grabbed me and planted a big kiss right on my mouth. I sputtered and ptooied to the best of my abilities, but the damage was done. The proletariat hoards were staring at us in dumbstruck horror, and I'd swear, the regulars never looked at me the same way after that.

Another unnerving episode took place at what was once the M.S.U. English Club's annual Elizabethan Dinner. The students had cajoled us professors into playing parts in Shakespeare's play within a play, Pyramus and Thisbee, and I had the ultimate privilege of playing Thisbee. Decked out in one of Judy's diaphanous peasant dresses, a flimsy shawl and a giant pair of galoshes, I falsettoed my way through the part, winding up prone on the stage, feebly kicking the huge galoshes in the air. After the applause had died down, I thought Richard was going to bust open he seemed so overjoyed. He came lumbering toward the stage, flush-faced, arms spread, shrieking and grinning and gave me a big hug and kiss—right there in front of all our English majors. I'm sure he would have given me a dozen red roses had they been available. Over her eye-rolling and foot-tapping, Judy said something like, "Shall we break out the condoms?" Richard told her that there was no need, but that the dress and galoshes had made me approximate the woman of his dreams.

Another more sinister night that I still hold in question as I look back took place at the Murray Hotel in Livingston shortly before Richard left Montana for the last time. He had been hugely depressed and alone at his house, so he had rented a room at the Murray where he could drink in town and stumble to a bed. I had come over to keep him company; so after some drinks, then a meal at the China Doll (which has since disappeared in a kitchen fire), some more drinks and a movie, *The Clash of the Titans* (which Richard called *The Clash of the Lips* because of Harry Hamlin's huge horrid lips), then some more drinks, after which the Captain said, "We need to stop by my room."

So we climbed the old stairs of the Murray, both of us slamming our heads into the low ceiling above the first flight and swearing all the way to his room. As soon as we got there, Richard turned on a little black and white T.V. full of fuzz and static, sat down on the bed and patted the spot next to him. I sat down and stared at the fuzzy little screen for a while but started to feel ill at ease. When I looked over at Richard, he was staring at me like he might stare at a cheeseburger. He said, "Welp, big guy?" and I said "Welp?" and got up, and he got up, and we stumbled downstairs, hitting our heads again near the landing, and proceeded on for a few more drinks. I have no idea what was up with that. Probably nothing.

But a couple of years earlier, in a fit of paranoia before he and Aki split, he accused me of wanting to fuck her. I had never harbored any such intention, but he continued on.

"You want to fuck her, and I'll tell you why you want to fuck her. Because you want to fuck me. I am a famous writer, and you want to fuck me, but you are afraid of such things, so you want to fuck my wife instead."

Later I was talking to Sean Garrity, a young friend of Richard's who helped him out at his place and, for a while, went out with Ianthe. He told me that the Captain had accused him of the same thing and that he had come that close (he held up a little space between his thumb and index finger) to decking him. It never really occurred to me that I might deck him, but I wondered what he must have been through to get such things in his head.

Perhaps part of the reason that Richard occasionally attacked his friends, or at least felt compelled to keep us ill at ease, was that he felt we should "pay" for his company. He wanted to dash any possibility that we were hanging out with him because of his celebrity.

Richard moons the camera man: "Something to remember me by."

As sort of a parting gesture of sexual ambiguity, to make me hesitate any time I thought of him, Richard gave me a picture of himself bearing his bottom in some sylvan setting in Bolinas. Next to him is some unknown comic who looks like he's giving directions to a heavy equipment operator. "Something to remember me by," is what he said, handing me the picture as I took him to the airport and his final departure from Montana.

The Restaurant at
the Bottom of the Night

Eating out with the Captain was often an intentional exercise in futility. Most of the time, food was something that had to be gotten out of the way, whether it was in the lurid lights of a truck stop or the flat glare of a McDonalds or Burger King. That's not to say we didn't both agree on the desired fare: chicken fried steak.

It would seem that type of cuisine wouldn't be hard to find in small-town Montana, but usually that raw hankering for hammered cube steak rolled in egg and flour became an epic quest ending in front of some tawdry heat-lamp-shrunk clam strips or a flying saucer made from a scoop of instant mashed potatoes with a ring of pickled crab apple around it.

The first time we ate out together was at the Sport Bar in Livingston. After what appeared to be a North Dakota burrito under a viscous green fluid that the waitress called guacamole arrived at our table and we stared at it for a while, I offered to get the tab. Richard immediately said, "You bet big guy. You'll learn."

And I did learn that Richard only got the tab when there were a lot of people around and he could look like a big spender.

Much of the time, I was surprised that Richard was so patient with the odd fare that appeared at our table. Chicken fried steak came out of the truck stop kitchen burned under a gelatinous white slick and he ate it with gusto. What seemed to be a salad of grapes, grape jello and nuts mixed with whipped cream and (I hope) chunks of celery came to our table from the Martin's Cafe kitchen, and Richard ate his portion AND mine after dubbing it dwarf vomit. Richard liked to use the word dwarf since his friend Peter Fonda had been in a total bomb of a movie called *Dance of the Dwarves.*

But once at the 4Bs restaurant in Bozeman, when Richard ordered eggs, a sausage patty and hash browns, and the sausage patty came out pink in the middle, it was as if someone had taken a pot shot at him. He started yelling at the waitress,

"It's raw! It's raw! You're trying to kill me!"

"Let me take a look," said the waitress, not knowing what she was getting into.

"What! Don't you believe me? Do you think that I am lying when I tell you that this thing you have placed in front of me is a breeding ground for trichina worms?"

"I guess it does look a little pink."

"You guess! You guess? You are serving us an active agent in a trichina delivery system and you GUESS!"

Since I hate confrontations, and I've always had a soft spot for waitresses, especially ones that have to work the night shift, I took the sausage patty from his plate and wolfed it down in a couple of bites.

"There, I guess that settles that. It was really very good. Thank you Lou Anne," I said, glancing up at her name tag.

Richard looked at me as if he expected me to explode. "You are a very foolish man. Can you feel the little cysts start to open up in you? Can you feel the worms eating their way through your organs?"

"Yes," I said. "And it feels pretty darned good if I do say so myself."

"Well, they're your organs, not mine. And I can always find myself another large fool to drive me around."

"Yes," I said, "there are many of us. There must be because the worms eat us so quickly."

Richard didn't say much after that, even when I left a large tip for Lou Anne.

The Captain's Kindnesses

Maybe Richard's occasional rudenesses pop back into memory so quickly because they were so sudden and unexpected, like a snake striking. His kindnesses were more subtle and formed enough of a balance that I and other friends were willing to endure what Richard called "He Who Dwells in Darkness," for a glimpse of what I called "Captain Belly-Buster," the smart compassionate clown. I guess in this way, he was pretty much of a coyote figure, an archetypal trickster who was bound to go off in any direction at any minute.

On the one hand, when I came up for tenure at M.S.U., things weren't looking so good for me because a previous department head had told me that none of my creative writing would count as publications, partially because there was no one in the vicinity to evaluate it. So when I took the huge chance of asking Richard for the favor of writing me a letter of support, he looked at me sadly and said that in the past any letters he'd written for friends had proven to be "the kiss of death," especially in academia. I didn't press the matter and went away sulking. Later, after I barely got tenure by writing a few scholarly articles in addition to my poetry, a new department head, Paul Ferlazzo, encouraged me to write an article for the *Dictionary of Literary Biography* on William Saroyan to raise my credibility with my peers.

I got pretty huffy about the whole idea and was fuming and ranting as Richard and I had a drink at the Eagles, but the Captain's ears perked up and he said, "William Saroyan, what a wonderful writer. This should be fun!" I looked at him skeptically since the last time I had said, "Are we having fun yet?" he had responded with, "Fun? What do you mean by this thing 'fun'. It is an odd concept to me, this word, 'fun'."

But before I knew it, he was giving me a detailed lecture on Saroyan's early years and his relationship with Martha Foley at *Story Magazine*–and on his own correspondences with this hub of modern fiction. He loaned me books, gave me insights and generally put a lot of time and effort into making sure I did a good job on the essay, partially, I imagine, because he would want someone to do a good job on his own entry in the DLB some day. My little piece on Saroyan was Richard's project–through me.

Richard also had a soft spot for kids who were having trouble. Though, in general, he never showed much interest in my boys, Chris and Max, when Chris, my stepson, came down with juvenile onset diabetes, he got busy researching the disease and was always dispensing advice, frequently helpful, on how Chris might deal with it and what problems Judy and I might have in getting him to check his blood and take his shots.

Another time, my colleagues Michael and Lynda Sexson's son, Devin, was having trouble adjusting to being an adolescent in Bozeman's conservative climate, so Richard suggested he, Michael and I take Devin fishing. Richard said his own adolescence was a living, breathing hell, so he seemed to tune right into Devin's state of mind. As I watched them talking and fishing on a pile of rocks by the Yellowstone, they looked like they had been cut out of the same cloth, both in their mannerisms and their looks. Richard had broken his leg a few months before and was still using a cane, so before we dropped Devin off, Richard gave him the cane. He frequently made such symbolic gestures that had both an immediate surface effect and, when considered later, a more profound significance. I'm pretty sure Devin still has that cane.

Sometimes when I'd go out to keep the Captain company at his house (and try to keep up with his drinking), I would follow him into the pits of despair where he would talk about the death of his friends—like Nikki, a Chinese American woman in the Bay area. He would never cry, but he would start choking on his words, then catch himself and turn cruel. Not necessarily toward me, but toward anyone whom he would normally trust and consider as a friend. He would lash out at his agent, his ex-wife Aki, the

Japanese in general, friends in the community, and then sometimes he would turn his sights on me until I felt I was right there at the end of the world with him. And just as I would be eying the door, ready for my permanent exit from this black vacuum, he would turn around and offer a profound kindness. At the end of one of these evenings when he had focused his rage on me–probably because I was the only person handy to focus it on–I was lurching toward my car and he came out and called me back.

"Wait," he said.

"Not likely," I said.

"I have something for you."

"Not likely," I said.

"It's a book."

"Just what I need," I said, "another book." I got into my car.

"It's the only one of its kind. I've signed it for you."

I got out of my car. "Why?" I said.

"Why is it the only one of its kind?" he said.

"No," I said, "why do you want to give it to me?"

"Because I am drunk and I have just insulted my friend."

"Oh," I said, and I walked back into the house with him.

The book was his author's copy of his new novel *So the Wind Won't Blow It All Away.* It is leather bound with a hard cover and an old fashioned design of swirling colored ink.

On the title page he has written

    Greg

              love

                           Richard

    I, of course, still have the book. I just now went to my bookcase to look at it and noticed two flaws on the back cover—two water spots. I'm not sure whether they're my tears or Richard's whisky. Maybe they're both.

Richard Brautigan

So the Wind Won't Blow It All Away

Greg

Love

Richard

Forest Park

Richard seemed to know when he was pressing his luck and getting on his friends' nerves, so when he knew I couldn't take much more, at least for a while, he'd find friends to keep him company. Among these were Marian Hjortsberg, Becky Fonda, Sean Cassidy, Karen "Scoop" Datko, Tandy Riddle, and perhaps, most of all Brad and Georgia Donovan. In the summer of 1982, he spent much of his Bozeman time out at their trailer in a place called Forest Park on the Gallatin River. I liked to visit the three of them out there because the trailer was right next to the river and I could set a baited rod and keep tabs on it through the window while we bullshitted inside.

Richard found this practice particularly delightful because it was such a typical tawdry example of my Oklahoma background. Also it seemed to fit right in with the fictions that fluttered around in the back of his mind. *So the Wind Won't Blow It All Away* had just come out in its trade edition, and on the cover was a couch placed next to a pond, an illustration of one of the episodes inside.

On one occasion, I was still smarting a little from some recent rudeness, so I was a little standoffish. He enjoyed teasing me when I was in these moods, so he swatted a mosquito on my back. Hard.

"What the hell was that for," I said.

"Just swatting a mosquito. Just takin' care of the big guy.

Am I making you nervous?"

"Yes."

"Good, nothing like a case of nerves to keep a big, slow Oklahoman on his toes."

I looked at him. When he was out at Forest Park, he tended to let himself go. He had a couple days worth of whiskers and smelled pretty funky, so I said, "You look just like a Bowery bum."

Richard seemed genuinely hurt, though usually he seemed to enjoy friends ribbing him. Sometimes I'd tell him he should eat more vegetables when he was on a drinking binge, or I would loan him a jean jacket and say it looked like a girdle on him (because, what with his pot belly, it did). "I'm on vacation," said Richard, stroking his stubble.

"No you're not," said Brad. "You're working. We're working."

"Yes, I can tell," I said. "The whole trailer is atremble with the bustle of industry."

"Tell him about the screenplay," said Georgia.

So Brad and Richard proceeded to tell me about their project, a screenplay, a possible pilot for a television series called, "Trailer." It involved a tank of mechanical goldfish, a dwarf, an old couple who wrapped themselves in tin foil and waited for aliens, a borrower who was constantly borrowing things—a whole plethora of wild and crazy residents of a trailer park similar to the one where we were sitting.

```
OPENING - EXTERIOR - TRAILER PARK - DAY                          2

With a dolly shot, the camera scans and establishes a trailer park.
One hears chain saws, dogs barking, and theme from "The Good, the
Bad, and the Ugly," a bulldozer, lots of birds, and, coming from
individual trailers, music that couldn't get aired if you held a gun
to the DJ's head.  For instance:  Slim Whitman, Mitch Miller, Mary
Martin singing "I'm Going to Wash that Man Right Out of My Hair,"
"76 Trombones," Bing Crosby singing "Tura Lura Lura," "Rain Drops
Keep Falling on My Head."

(VO)
        Let the dog out.

        I let the dog out last time.

        I'm tired of arguing about the dog.

                                        CUT TO

A trailer window, complete with window box and flowers.  The window
opens and a Lassie-type dog comes flying out.

Out of his trailer comes the Borrower.  He borrows things from the
occupants of the trailer park for no apparent reason.  They never
refuse him.  The brief scenes that get him in and out of all the
other characters' trailers provide lyrical transitions.  The Borrower
is capable of a sort of saintly charm, and at other times an energy
belonging to Rasputin.

We see Borrower walking distractedly through the morning.  Out of
another trailer steps Lee, as in Van Cleef, carrying a chain saw.

                        BORROWER
        Good morning, Lee.
        (Lee squints.)
```

An excerpt from a television screenplay called "Trailer."

For the next couple of weeks, the two of them worked frantically on the screenplay. I think Richard had imagined some sort of deadline, or maybe he was just planning to return to Bolinas. Whatever the case was, the project seemed to have a life and death urgency about it, so that toward the end they were both getting a little testy. To calm their nerves, I took them out to a small pond next to the Bozeman shopping mall, sat them down and made them watch me catch worn out hatchery trout the size of small dogs. I even started writing them a ditty for the project called "A Song to Go." It was basically a description of Forest Park ambience, but I didn't get it finished before they finished "Trailer" and Richard left. In fact, he never heard it, but to me and Brad it became sort of a requiem for the Captain. Here it is.

A Song To Go

(for Richard and Brad)

Dreamin' of bikinis and eatin' beany weenies
And tunin' into "Fantasy Island."
Collectin' unemployment's afternoon enjoyments
Only way to keep you smilin'.
You heard the presidenté say there'll be peace and plenty
Waitin' if he's re-elected.
But you can only understand if there's a whisky in your hand,
And the telephone is disconnected.

Chorus:

> *Good morning, sailor, did you dream that you woke up,*
>
> *Or was that a song that you heard on the radio?*
>
> *Good morning, sailor, here's some coffee for your cup*
>
> *And a song to go.*
>
> *Look into the mirror to see if you're still here.*
>
> *Suck your gut in and pull back your shoulders.*
>
> *Put a Roll-Aids on your tongue and pretend that you're still young,*
>
> *Though the mirror says you're getting older.*
>
> *Cook a T.V. dinner and forget that you're a sinner,*
>
> *And the end could come most any day now.*
>
> *Yes, forget about religion, take a beer out of the fridge an'*
>
> *Let that song inside your head start to play now.*

Chorus

> *Findin' bargains on bologna and payin' alimony*
>
> *And stoppin' in to check the mail box.*
>
> *There's a bill from Roto Rooter and a leaflet on computer*
>
> *Training if you're willing to pay lots.*
>
> *And when the bars all close up you ask 'em for a go-cup*
>
> *And nurse it till you see the morning.*
>
> *Then you call yourself a dreamer and stir non-dairy creamer*
>
> *In another cup of coffee while you sing.*

Chorus

A Xerox of "Trailer" is still in a box out in my garage somewhere.

I think it was that same summer when Jenny and Ed Dorn came to Forest Park with their children, Kidd and Maya, to see Richard, Brad and Georgia. During the visit, Kidd caught a big rainbow trout (his first) near the trailer. I wasn't there at the time, but apparently the Captain was so thrilled that he cackled and wheezed about it all the way through the Livingston Rodeo that they attended that afternoon. I mention this because in the only photograph of Richard at Forest Park, he is standing (or perhaps I should say wobbling) behind Kidd and his trout, tickled pink.

PHOTO BY GEORGIA DONOVAN

Left to right: Jenny Dorn, Brad Donovan, Kid Dorn, Ed Dorn, Maya Dorn, Richard admire Kid Dorn's first trout.

The Range Hotel

Tokyo, May 6, 1984

Dear Greg,
There is a possibility that I will be pulling up stakes and heading back to the US soon. Alert the boys to wake up their liver.

Who knows?
Richard

PS I don't think I would have left Montana if they hadn't closed the Range Hotel.

After the quarter he spent teaching at M.S.U., Richard had made several friends in Bozeman and was lonely staying out at his place, so he moved into the Range Hotel on Bozeman's Main Street, just a few buildings down from the Eagles Bar and three blocks from my house. Now, of course, the place has been gentrified.

Before Richard's death, it was converted to a brokerage. I don't know what's there now, and I don't particularly want to know.

When Richard was living at the Range, it was a pretty amazing place and was literally occupied by retired cowboys, ranchers, and blue-collar workers, who sat around in the lobby in worn out chairs with canes or crutches propped next to them. Dick Dillof got a place there too, so, between him and Richard, there was frequently a mood of wacky desperation which seemed to invigorate the old guys in the lobby. It was paradise for Richard—cheap, authentic, next to his favorite bar, and near his friends. I liked it too. He didn't need me to drive him around, and I could visit him whenever I wanted to. As Richard said in his usual dark prophetic way before he knew The Range would be closed, "All in all, the place is DOOMED." There is, however, a lasting legacy. Richard started a book while he was there called *American Hotels,* and I've heard rumors that the yellow legal pad manuscript is lying under wraps somewhere.

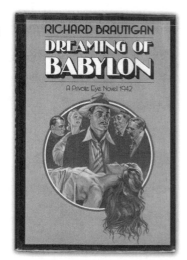

Fishing

For the Captain, fishing was usually past or future tense. The equipment, the flies, etc., were in the present. He had a glass rod, light as a weed and he liked to hold it out and shake it slightly then pass it to the person next to him to experience the proper awe. The flies he used were also next to nothing, size 16 to 20. Most of the time, this wonderful tackle sat in the washroom.

But there were those rare occasions when we would actually put the equipment in the back of my Mazda station wagon, and go out to a local stream. One such excursion was to the Yellowstone about a mile behind Richard's house. He was in a twinkling mood because he had just sold the film options for *Dreaming of Babylon* to actress Kate Jackson of *Charlie's Angels* fame. Maybe that and the cool, clear weather got him out from behind the Dickel, into my car, and down a dirt road to the river. Taking his stuff out of the back, he hit his head on the swing-up tailgate so that he bled a little. But it didn't seem to phase him. As we squeaked and wallowed down the bank in our huge, clown-like chest waders, we commented on what the Japanese must have intended when they built cars with tailgates like that and sold them to big lumbering Americans.

Richard waded upstream and fished the slower water inside a big riffle on a bend in the river with a tiny dark nymph. I waded downstream a ways where the water was straight and fast and lobbed a big spoon toward the deep blue-green near the undercut of the far bank. Richard looked down at me from where he was fishing. He never fished with anything but flies–at least as an adult. Once he told me that he used to fish salmon eggs to carp where the sewage came into a river in Tacoma. He said he could actually see flecks of toilet paper among the wallowing carp. But apparently he'd left that kind of behavior behind with his youth, or maybe that was the only part of his youth that he had left behind. Actually, fishing salmon eggs to toilet paper carp still sounds pretty good to me. I've never gotten over my childish infatuation with bait and lures, though I'll fish with flies if they happen to be working better.

After a while, the Captain caught a couple of nice whitefish. Local fishermen usually throw whitefish up on the bank and let them rot, but not Richard. He had seen too many of them smoked and selling for many dollars a pound in the Bay area. He had also seen Japanese friends go ape-shit when they got their hands on a whitefish. No sir, these whitefish were immediately cleaned and popped in my creel which I had left up on the bank near him. He called my creel "The Death Bag" since he knew how much meat had passed through it. Soon, I was fooling some rainbow trout in the deep water with my big hunk of metal. Since I didn't have my creel, I just threw them up on the bank in a sort of frenzy. After a while, I turned to deal with the flopping fish, but Richard was already there, clonking each fish very precisely on the head with a small rock. "You should kill them quickly," he said with a smile of mild accusation.

Later, I filleted the trout and Richard put the whitefish in for smoking. I have a smoker in my back yard made from a converted refrigerator. Richard called it Auschwitz. Smoked fish were always an integral part of our relationship. Sometimes he'd have me send boxes of smoked fish express mail to people like Shiina Takako, his Japanese sister in Tokyo, or Terry Gardiner, the "wild legislator" in Ketchikan, Alaska. And sometimes that worked out pretty well for me. Once Shiina Takako sent me a box of ayu, a rare Japanese fish, preserved in a delicate oil. But Terry Gardiner never responded. I have a feeling that he might have come home from some political junket to find a package of smoked trout rotting in his mailbox.

Perhaps the most idyllic trip we ever took was to Bridger Creek just outside the Bozeman city limits. Richard really liked small streams, maybe because they seemed more magical, and the fish that come out of these streams are almost always harder, crisper, and brighter in color. We waded just upstream from a small irrigation dam and started flailing. This time, Richard had shamed me into bringing my fly rod, so we were more or less on even footing. Richard was using about a size 18 white gnat-like fly and I was using some crude thing I'd made by tying frazzled chunks of nylon to small hooks, but the fish didn't seem to care what we threw at them. They were so hungry we probably would have done pretty well using rabbit shit. We must have caught and released ten or fifteen fish apiece (Yes, I said released; Richard shamed me into that too.) before the land owner came down and ran us off. Richard may have had his way on using flies and releasing fish, but I still managed to drag him into one of my foul fishing practices. As we left, he said, "You see, Greggie, you're supposed to ask permission," in a tone quite similar to the previous, "You should kill them quickly."

But most of my fishing trips with the Captain had very little to do with fishing. They usually went something like this: Richard would call me around nine or ten in the morning and say, "Let's go fishing." Since he knew that I was always suspicious of this midmorning suggestion, he would throw in something like "I know the perfect spot on Trail Creek" or "Go ahead and bring some sculpins too. I won't mind." And when he knew he had my interest, he would say, "Oh, and on your way, stop and buy some George Dickel. I'll pay you back."

Photo by Greg Keeler
Richard's house from the backyard.

Of all these suggestions, usually the only one which transpired was my buying the Dickel. When I got to the ranch, the Dickel would be opened for "just a quick snort for the road." But soon the road would lead to his back porch and long painful discussions of his divorce, his water rights, the teen-agers who had "vandalized" his barn, and the black hole where money-grubbing publishers live, the question of whether or not to marry Masako and have a hit squad of Japanese-American kids, the doppleganger cat which had invaded his ranch, the mutant potatoes in his garden, or the deer that wandered near his barn. As we stared at the sky and mountains turning gold through our Dickel, his words drifted out in the air among the cottonwood seeds which always seemed to be there in warm weather, as if his ranch were suspended in one of those shakeup water balls.

By dark, fishing was usually somewhere on another planet, and I would wind up driving the mountain passes back to Bozeman at two or three in the morning, drunk and depressed. But by midmorning, I would hear again the merry jingle of my telephone, and it would be the Captain. "Let's go fishing tomorrow. Really."

The fishing trips that Richard and I planned in detail but never went on were probably the most interesting. Because of his fascination with small streams, he always liked the creeks in the Bozeman city limits. One of them, Bozeman (Sourdough) Creek, runs right under the Eagles Bar (about two blocks from my house) where he spent most of his drinking time here. Once while we were walking from the Eagles to my house, we saw a little girl pull a brook trout that weighted almost a pound out from under a tire store. That really got him going. He wondered how fishing was under the Eagles Bar, under Main Street, or in Bogart Park next to my house. The only obstacle in our way to finding out was a law restricting fishing within the city limits to children under the age of twelve.

Later, over Dickel in the Eagles, our plan began to take shape. We would make plywood cutouts of barefoot boys with straw hats and weeds in their teeth and hide behind them while we fished. We were so proud of our plan that we decided we should bring a photographer along and publish our expedition in some classy magazine like *Gray's Sporting Journal.* Of course, the plan never materialized. Now, I guess, if I'm going to follow through with it. I will have to make plywood cutouts of both a kid and Richard.

The last, and now, under the circumstances, the saddest fishing trip the Captain and I ever planned was to take place in the Bay area in August. I was teaching summer school at M.S.U. in Bozeman when I got a letter from Richard letting me know he was in Bolinas:

June 8, 1984

Dear Greg,

Fooled you! doubled back, returned to America, and I'm out here in my house in Bolinas where I plan on spending the summer before returning to Montana in the fall. There's a lot of work I want to do and I think this is a good place to do it. It's interesting to be back in America, but you knew that all the time, anyway.

Love,

Richard

Glad to know he was back and hoping Montana wasn't too far in his future, I wrote him a letter pissing and moaning about my teaching and telling him that I would be playing songs at an anti gold mining fundraiser in Nevada City, California in June. Gary Snyder and the people who were putting it on were paying to fly me down and back to Bozeman, so there was really no way I could visit the Captain. I had to get right back for classes. But anyway, he wrote me the following:

June 15, 1984

Dear Greg,

I just got your letter. You poor sack of shit!

I don't have a telephone and may not get one, but my neighbor does and he'll come over and get me if somebody calls. His number is ___ ___ ____. I use his telephone sparingly, so don't spread it all over the landscape of Montana. That's an interesting vision: Greggie wandering all over Montana, spreading ___ ___ ____ on everything he comes across: dogs, trees, rocks, etc.

Anyway, O unhappy one, I sure would like to see you. We'll get together for certain when you come down in July. Any chance in June? It's only a few more fucking hours down from Nevada City. I know somebody out here who's got a salmon boat docked a few hundred yards away.

It's something to think about.

Let me know.
Don't be afraid of the telephone number.

Love,
Richard

Since I was going to the Bay area to visit my brother in late July
and early August, I knew I would be seeing Richard, so I decided to
get feisty. I knew his M.O. He was just trying to lure me over for
Dickel drinking. Besides, one of my friends had told me that El Ñino
had wiped out most of the salmon fishing in the Bay area for a long
time. So I wrote him back saying he'd have to get up awflly early
in the morning to fool a wiley Oklahoman: I knew that the salmon
fishing was shot. I wound up my letter with a hypothetical "Ancient
Mariner" story which ended something like "Niño Niño everywhere and all the salmon shrank," and he responded as follows:

June 23, 1984

Dear Greg,
The next time I pull a salmon out of the beautiful cold
waters of the Pacific Ocean, I'll say, "This one is for
Greggie. A loser in Montana."

Love from the deck,
Richard

After that letter, I made some feeble response, knowing that I was fencing with a master of ridicule and said that we would solve the salmon question when I came down to visit my brother. Richard's next response was to the point:

July 2, 1984

Dear Loser (formerly known as Greggie):
Dream on...
Losers tend to have loser friends.
"She says...
El Niño...changed...currents...salmon...moved...out."
That was last year.
It's nice to have good friends, loser. Excuse me while I have this delightful young girl place another bite of freshly-caught salmon in my jaws. Thank you, dear.
No, we'll do that later again. You can rest for a while, honey.
Now, where was I? O, yes, writing to a loser.
Excuse me again—
No honey, I don't have losers for friends, this one is a special case. Don't worry your pretty little head about it.
"She says...El Niño...changed...currents...salmon...moved out..."
Yes, yes, yes.
Meester Keeler. Why not do you geet me a salmon?!!!
[a spot on the paper with an arrow to it and a note]

(Caused by another bite of salmon being put in my mouth)

Love,
Richard

Of course, when I got to the Bay area, the number Richard had given me didn't exactly work like a charm. I called the people at the number and they said they'd leave my message and number for Richard. But somehow, after a week or so of back and forth message leaving, we still hadn't talked. In the meantime, my car had broken down and was in the most expensive garage in San Francisco (since they were the only ones who could find parts for it); my oldest son, Chris, had been picked up and released by the Moonies; and the salmon were definitely biting like crazy. I sat down by the Berkeley pier and watched Japanese tourists come in from charter boats with huge bags of them.

Finally, I got through to the Captain, and he said, "Here's the plan. I have this friend, Bob, in Stinson Beach who has a hot rod salmon boat with a couple of great big motors in it. We'll come down from Bolinas to Fisherman's Wharf in it, pick you up there, go out and murder salmon, then bring them back to North Beach and have my friend who owns a Japanese restaurant prepare them especially for us." Of course, as it turned out, Bob's boat wasn't working right, and the Japanese restaurant owner loaned Richard his .44 magnum.

The Ghost of
Richard Brautigan
on Trail Creek

Trail Creek where?

And what was he using?

Flies tied from spun diamond?

Did he know the algebra

of the stones?

Was his hair its

usual silly gold?

Did he fall and fill

his purple polka-dot

waders? Did his words

hover over pools

like clouds of midges?

No?

Then there's still hope.

Ode to Melancholy

I suppose, even though he spent much of his time denying or ridiculing the fact, Richard was an incurable romantic. I read somewhere that Ginsberg or Ferlinghetti dubbed him Bunthorne after the ethereal, languishing character in a Gilbert and Sullivan operetta. Richard himself was merciless when it came to poking fun at romantic characters, but at heart, he was among their ranks.

When we used to drink at the Robin (back then, the only watering hole in Bozeman approximating a fern bar), we would occasionally see a solitary young man dressed in black, hunched in a dark corner with coffee, earnestly scribbling away on a note pad, and Richard would say, "Look, a melancholic!"

"A what?"

"You know, a melancholic. A Bozeman melancholic."

"You mean like in Burton's "The Anatomy of Melancholy?""

"No, I mean like yonder earnest young man, gloomily scrawling away in his little pad."

"You mean Bill, the guy in the black coat–there in the corner?

"No, his name is not Bill. His name is Lord Byron. His name is Percy Shelly. His name is Faust. Notice the way his collar is turned up, the way he glances abstractly out the window."

"Maybe he's bored."

"No, no! How could you mistake true angst, the full weight of this 'I-fall-on-the-thorns-of-life-I-bleed' world for boredom!"

"Maybe his girl dumped him."

"Yes, yes, there you have it. He has been jilted in love and he must record the pain for posterity. It has driven him to abstraction. He must WRITE! Look at him grit his little teeth. Look at the furious movement of his little pen."

"I think I need another drink."

Though I had no doubts that the Captain was using a sardonic tone in his praise of melancholics, I also had no doubt that he had been just such a young man and, deep down, probably still was, for up to his death, Richard was always a fool for love.

Before I met him, Judy had seen him walking down Bozeman's Main Street with Aki. She was wearing a plaid mini skirt, a green sweater, and cowboy boots. Judy knew immediately that the couple must be the Brautigans because Richard looked like–well–Richard, and Aki looked like she had just stepped out of his novel *Sombrero Fall-Out*. He was always crazy about her. When I visited him in Bolinas, a couple of weeks before his death, he said he had seen her in San Francisco, walking down the street. He was obviously torn up about it.

After their divorce, he lived the rest of his life with a huge hole in his chest. He tried to fill the hole with whisky, writing, friends, other women, and frantic trips between Montana, Bolinas, and Tokyo, but it never went away until he put a smaller hole in his head.

That's not to say his life was over when the marriage ended. He managed to squeeze in a few interesting years and get what was left of his heart broken at least once more before his death.

Even in the months after she left, Richard managed to maintain his twisted sense of humor. In several phone calls from the apartment in San Francisco, he'd recount surreal tales of sudden bachelorhood. Around three one morning, he awoke in front of his television in time to hear Gabby Hayes yell, "Why, she's got Californy fever!" To Richard, this seemed like the ultimate existential commentary on what had happened with Aki.

Another time he called to tell me that there was a derelict smashing a trash can lid against his head in the alley next to him, and he compared him to the club-footed man Madam Bovary heard outside of her house before she poisoned herself. After that, he called to tell me that a guy with a ring through his nipple had sat down next to him on a bus coming over the Golden Gate, and he had then decided that he'd better get back to Montana, fast.

He also said that he had gotten one of his brawnier friends to promise to break his leg if he ever got married again. When Richard arrived here, his leg was broken, but it had been an accident. I believe he said he had tripped over some furniture while attempting to turn off his television, but the injury was definitely a cosmic warning.

When a beautiful young Japanese woman, Masako, came back with him from a his summer residency in Boulder, I and several other friends shook our heads in disbelief. She was just a kid in her early twenties. She seemed like such an obvious attempt to replace Akiko. But the more I was around her, the more I realized that she was her own person and she and Richard really liked each other. I remember two particular occasions when I accompanied them on jaunts in the Livingston area. They both involved fishing.

The first was a trip to the Livingston Clinic. I was taking Richard and her to see our friend Dr. Dennis Noteboom for some reason that the Captain wouldn't disclose to me. Whatever the mission, my main memory is of fishing near the clinic. The Yellowstone River runs directly behind the building, so while Richard and Masako were at their clandestine rendezvous with Dennis, I was fishing out back with some Woolly Buggers I had just tied.

By some fluke, I caught a really nice brown trout while they watched me out the window. This in itself might not have been worthy of recalling, but our dialogue when they emerged from the clinic was.

"Did you kill it, big guy?"

"Kill what?"

"Big fish," she said. "Did you kill big fish?"

"How did you know I caught one?"

"We watch you through window."

"Besides," said the Captain, "your Death Bag is bulging." He pointed to Judy's old brown suede L.L. Bean purse which I had long since converted to a creel. It was wet and sagging with the recent catch.

"It was badly hooked," I lied. "I had to keep it."

"Hmmm, funny how they always get 'badly' hooked when YOU catch them. How shall we punish this large man, my pretty?"

"We eat the fish, O.K.?"

On another trip, the three of us piled in my tiny station wagon and headed east from Livingston up to Mission Creek where it runs near John Fryer's cabin toward the Yellowstone. (John runs Sax and Fryer's Book Store in Livingston, and Richard used to have a letter from John on his wall regarding the publication of his work. I think John's small town store was Richard's ideal of how his books should be sold.) It was late summer and the creek was low and clear, so the fish were spooky. When Richard and I donned our large clown-pants chest waders, Masako couldn't stop laughing.

"Do you find something humorous?" said Richard.

"Large water pants. Small water," said Masako.

"Come sit on my large water pants lap, and we will watch this large Oklahoman try to fish."

So I proceeded to stumble up and down the little stream in front of them, losing a couple #12 Hank Roberts Specials in the surrounding willows, getting my hair tangled in rose hip bushes, falling and banging my shin on a rock, swearing, etc. Eventually I lurched back to the outcropping where Masako was attempting to make bunny ears out of Richard's hair.

"Your turn, Captain Bunny," I said.

"Do you think there is a fish within a mile of this spot that isn't hiding in horror?" said Richard.

"Probably not."

"My bunny is hungry," said Masako.

So we went back to the house and made spaghetti.

For all that he had been through with his divorce, Richard seemed very happy when he was around Masako, but, just by looking at the two of them together, I could see doom. He was so big and old and American and she was so tiny and young and Japanese. So, sure enough, soon I was driving over the pass at odd hours to hear him lurch about his house in despair.

"Her parents are very traditional."

"Yes, I know."

"They are against us."

"Yes, I know."

"She will obey them."

"Yes."

"She is back in Japan."

"Yes, she lives there."

"I won't see her again."

"Probably not."

"Why do these things happen to me?"

"I don't know."

"I'll get us some whisky."

"O.K."

Eunice Kittigawa was another woman Richard really liked during the time I knew him. She grew up in Hawaii on Maui where, the last I heard, her mother ran a Benihanna's Restaurant. The Captain loved Eunice as a friend and sometimes almost as a sister. Of all Richard's female companions, I found Eunice the easiest to get along with.

Perhaps Richard did too because he flew to Hawaii and spent several months with her in Honolulu one winter. He sent me a photograph from there of himself holding a fighting cock and wearing a tee shirt with a chicken in an army tank on it. I think the caption was something like "fighting chickens." In the Captain's posthumous novel, *An Unfortunate Woman,* that picture plays a pivotal role.

PHOTO BY EUNICE KITTIGAWA

Richard in Hawaii, holding a fighting cock.

At any rate, Richard might have cashed 'em in much sooner if it hadn't been for Eunice. She was so kind and considerate, Lord knows what she must have gone through during the Captain's late night "the horror, the horror" sessions. After Richard left, both she and Masako sent me pictures of themselves and letters and kept corresponding even after he died.

Ode to the Melancholic

"She dwells with Beauty—Beauty that must die"

—John Keats

Put down that Dickel, drop that .44.
The true connoisseur takes his heartache
full-on. Were you less alive before
you knew her than you are now? So take
all that sorrow and glut it on a rainbow
trout or a river full of light. Women—
to you, they're only beautiful when they go
away or die, and joy's only joy when
you know it's going to turn to shit. Time
leaks out of the clock and poisons all the flowers.
You there, hiding in your little shrine
of bullet holes, don't try to trade your hours
for sleep. You'd just as well hang your soul
on a bowling trophy as lose it on a girl.

Me and Captain Death

If readers of his fiction think Richard himself may have been preoccupied with death, they're right. He was a great admirer of Hemingway, and in some of his gloomier moments, he would read aloud the bleak, concise descriptions of death between the short stories of *In Our Time*. He knew when, how, why, and with what kind of weapon Hemingway killed himself. He knew the battles and carnage of the Civil War by heart. He quoted Picket's comment about Lee: "That damned old man killed all of my men." When I would drive him home down the East River Road, he would point to the crosses marking accidents and tell stories about how they happened. Near the Deep Creek Bridge he would talk about an accident that was so brutal a young woman's panties were left hanging in the high branches of a tree. With his usual morbid humor, when we passed the place, he would sometimes mutter, "Ah, Panty-Tree Bridge." When we drove by a little cemetery, he told a story about how the proprietor had run out of space and was caught stashing corpses in a shed. Sometimes he would call me in loneliness and desperation to come out and drink with him because the ghosts of old lovers were haunting him and all he had to combat them was the "hollow clomping of his feet" as he roamed the house.

The summer before he left the area, he and Marian had a falling out because a horse had died on the land behind her house. Instead of having it buried, she wanted to let nature take care of the animal. This horrified Richard, and he made a huge drunken scene about it. I wasn't there, but I think he was actually going to stumble down the brushy, boulder-strewn hill drunk that night and try to bury it himself.

Because he had been involved in a project with the Beatles, he knew and liked John Lennon. I think that he felt that they had a lot in common, and when Lennon was murdered, he felt that he had been moved a little closer to death—on a grand scale. When his Chinese-American friend Nikki died, it devastated him, and he became drawn and gaunt, skipping meals and staring off of his back porch for hours.

Sometimes, when I would need a break from the alcohol and the death talk, I would leave Richard to stew on his own—and later feel awful about it because, if he didn't find other companions, he'd spiral into a physical and psychological oblivion. During his teaching stint at M.S.U., he'd hobble drunk with his cane and broken leg from bar to bar around the freezing icy streets of

Bozeman, getting a lift back to his room bouncing around in the back of some cowboy's pick up, though, when I'd take him up to campus for his class the next day, he'd rub snow on his face and undergo a sort of miraculous transformation into lucidity.

In 1983, after a long flight to Japan on Korean Air Lines, (one of whose jets had just been shot down by the Russians), he wrote me this letter. I thinks it's typical of his Mr. Death attitude, both grim and humorous:

Tokyo, April 23, 1983

Dear Greg,
Well, I'm Here. It was a long trip and I'm still getting over the jet lag. In two days I flew 10,079 miles into the sun. After a while I was no longer human. I was just meat flying 600 miles an hour. My childhood vanished into hamburger and all the memories of my life were just chunks hanging from a flying hook.

I think I want to stay on the ground for a while.

Love,
Richard

He told me that during a visit to Amsterdam in 1984, for a conference concerning that Orwellian year, he had met a woman in a grocery store and accompanied her to Spain where she grew tired of his antics and abandoned him. I think he said it was in Barcelona where he found himself lying in an alley behind a bodega, sleeping among dogs. After he somehow made it to Tokyo, he sent me a death-warmed-over photo-booth snapshot of himself and his letter.

Tokyo, Feb. 14, 1984

Dear Greg,
You have probably looked at the photograph of me taken just before my birthday. Yes, Europe has been good to me.

Love,
Richard

PS Send T-Shirts Airmail. And tell Brad where I'm at and to send T Shirts

I'm not sure whether he consciously admired the archetype of the dark, perishing, misunderstood Romantic hero or whether it was just in his genes. He once told me about seeing Jack Kerouac in Big Sur. Richard was in a bar (of course) and noticed a drunk passed out under the urinal. He asked his friend, "Who's that?" and his friend said, "That's Jack Kerouac." When he told me this story, he seemed to light up—as if passing out under a urinal was, in a sense, one of the top things a guy could do.

Here's a tiny screenplay that condenses much of Captain Death's persona into a single episode, (even though Richard, like Truman Capote, believed that screenplays are just "typing."

Scene opens with a steady-cam shot from a car traveling at night up the East River Road. It is one in the morning in mid-January and huge snakes of fog are trailing down in front of the Absoroka Mountains into the snow-covered valley, all illuminated by a full moon.

Captain Death: Where's my go-cup?

Greg: I think you put it on the floor and knocked it over. Can't you smell it?

Captain Death: To me, everything smells like whisky. I think I have some old Jim Beam left at home, from when those FM Tokyo boys were visiting.

Greg: More whisky?

Captain Death: More whisky.

Greg: Richard Hugo died last week.

Captain Death: Yes, I know. He was a good poet. Did you say he stopped drinking for a couple years before he died?

Greg: Sort of.

Captain Death: Up there (he points above the Absorokas), that cloud looks like a huge vulture!

Cut to interior of Captain Death's house where he and Greg are sitting at the kitchen table with tumblers of whisky.

Greg: Now that Hugo is dead, everyone will be scrambling to publish his work, his letters–like feeding vultures. (He makes his hand into a vulture and circles it in the air in front of him making vulture noises.) Ree, ree, ree!

Captain Death: That's what they do all right. When you're alive, they see you as a perpetual language pump. Your words are a dime a dozen. But when you die, you are meat–and here they come, ree, ree, ree!

Greg: Ree, ree, ree!

Captain Death: When I'm alive, they call my work "pet rock fiction." They dismiss my work as that of a washed up hippy. My home turf, *The San Francisco Chronicle,* hires a hatchet woman to trivialize my life. But when I die, it will be ree, ree, ree!

Greg: Ree, ree, ree!

Captain Death: But I would never end my own life to make my work into valuable carrion.

Greg: No?

Captain Death: No, I wouldn't want friends to have to clean up the actual mess.

Greg: But no matter how you die, the vultures will be there to clean up on your work. Ree, ree, ree.

Captain Death: (standing up and frowning at Greg) It appears that you think this matter is funny.

Greg: No, I just....

Captain Death: It appears that you find death humorous. (He points up at a kitchen clock that's peppered with bullet holes.) My friend and I shot that clock full of holes. It seemed appropriate at the time.

Greg: Why?

Captain Death: Because time is not funny, just like death is not funny.

Greg: I think I'd better be going.

Captain Death: You will betray me, just as they all betray me.

Greg: Do I have a choice in the matter?

Captain Death: No.

Exit Greg. Lights dim on Captain Death sitting alone at the table with his tumbler of whisky.

Funny

Whenever I spoke of something being fun or funny, Richard either wouldn't respond or would act as if the words were some kind of hex, maybe because he sometimes saw language as a way of killing spontaneity or maybe because his humor was so deeply tied to his depression. That's not to say he didn't appreciate slapstick. Once at the Oaks Bar in Bozeman, (long since replaced by an art gallery), we were in what I thought was a serious conversation and he picked up a bowl of pop corn and dumped it on his head saying, "Look, a North Dakota blizzard." Occasionally, I'd try to spring some locker room humor on him. When he'd fart, I might say something like, "Lord, let's get out of here before it consumes us both," and he'd ignore me and glumly go on with what he was doing. But when we were drinking at the Eagles, and I seriously suggested that he might consider eating more vegetables, he'd start shrieking in uncontrollable laughter.

Richard liked to laugh at me a lot, especially when I had no idea I was being funny. It wasn't a cruel laughter but more of a spontaneous reaction to innocence in the face of experience, as if William Blake's lamb were trying to act natural in front of his tyger. While we were at a table eating hamburgers at the Eagles' burger-nite Friday, the Captain might come out with something like this:

"You like that there burger, big guy?"

"Uh huh, I guess."

"That's some burger-grip you've got there."

"Yes, I hold it that way so I can eat it."

"Oh, (laughter) so that's what you're doing with it. The way you're holding it, I thought it might be a religious ritual." (more laughter)

"No, I'm just eating it."

"Welp, they're awfully big. There's lot's of chaos in that burger—loose lettuce, slippery tomatoes, blunt onions."

"Blunt?"

"Eat up, big guy. Our burger's getting cold, and we wouldn't want that now would we." (laughter)

"Maybe if we weren't having to talk, we would find it easier to eat."

"Watch out!" A piece of lettuce falls on my plate and he snatches it up. (shrieking) "Looks like a lettuce disaster. I'm losing my respect for your burger grip."

"Glmmph."

"Enjoying your burger?"

"Mmmph."

"I hate to break it to you, but a piece of pickle is slipping. I may have to stop hanging out with you. It's too humiliating, what with the slipping pickle and all."(shriek)

"Would you please pass the mustard?"

"Please!" (laughter) "Please! I'm glad to hear the big guy's mother raised him right."

"The mustard."

"But of course, please forgive me. And perhaps you would like some salt? Some pepper? (shriek) Some ketchup?" He whisks each before me as he asks the question.

"No."

"No? Did I just hear the big guy say no? But where's the thank you?

"Perhaps in Oklahoma, mothers teach their sons to say please, but I'm afraid they haven't advanced to the thank you stage yet." (Fading laughter.)

Even in his darker moments (if I could detach enough), Richard himself was flat out funny: the way he'd wobble around on his cowboy boots when he walked, the way he'd lurch purposefully with his hands clasped behind him when he was preoccupied, the way he'd encounter sudden physical pain with no emotion as if it were some alien sensation.

But most of all, I appreciated how the Captain could make any word funny just by saying it or writing it with proper timing. Here's a letter he wrote me from Tokyo after I had a hernia operation:

Tokyo, April 9, 1984

Dear Greg,
I hope your guts are OK, but I don't know why [you] got an operation. What's wrong with standard Oklahoma treatment: an intertube [sic]? Can't see no trout out this window. Always look on the bright side, if your gut operation backfires, which they often do, you can use yourself as bait.

Thinkin' real hard about the big boy,

Richard

The Captain Gives a Reading

During his teaching residency in the spring of '82, Richard had volunteered to give a reading as part of his job. I was a little nervous about it because few of the faculty seemed to care much about Richard's poetry and much of the Bozeman community in general seemed about as interested in poetry as they would be in a cinder block. I was somehow hoping that students or some local organization would publicize the event, so, shortly before the reading, when he asked who was doing the publicity and I said I didn't know, he blew a gasket.

"Some agent you'd make," he said.

"I know," I said. "I'm a horrible agent. I don't even know what an agent does."

"Obviously. Well, it's not too late. Let's go get the posters and put them up. I can't believe I'm going to have to do this myself."

"Posters?"

"Yes, the posters."

"What posters?"

"What the fuck kind of place is this?"

"It's a state university in Montana."

So somehow we made up some posters and dashed, or I should say hobbled and lurched, madly around campus and Bozeman in general, putting them up in store windows and on poles, trees and bulletin boards. It was a pretty primitive pre-computer poster as I remember, what with its hand-scrawled letters, ditto paper, etc. I was worried that just a few huddled liberals and coerced students would show up and groan knowingly or sulk after each poem as had happened at other infrequent readings.

When we drove, hobbled and lurched out to the new shopping mall on the west end of town, I had a sense of impending doom and futility. Especially when we entered the B. Dalton's to put up a poster and the clerk hadn't heard of his work.

"Do you have any of Richard Brautigan's work?" said Richard.

"What does he write?" said the clerk.

"He writes novels and books of poetry." Richard's mouth was assuming an odd shape under his moustache.

"What kind of novels?" said the clerk.

"Famous ones, you know, like great literature," said Richard without moving his mouth very much because his teeth were gritted.

"Our literary works are over there, and our poetry section is over there," said the clerk, pointing first to a large part of the wall near us then to a tiny clump of books in the back of the store.

"Thank you," gritted Richard.

Soon we had scoured both sections and found one book, The Hawkline Monster, in the whole store, so the Captain returned to the clerk while I hung back.

"I would like to give you a little lesson in capitalism," said Richard. I am Richard Brautigan. I write novels and books of poetry. People like them. When stores stock them, people buy them. You only have one of my books because people bought the rest of them. But you do not stock more of them. That is how book stores make money. People come to them to buy books, and in return, they give the book stores money. DON'T YOU FUCKERS WANT TO MAKE SOME FUCKING MONEY!!!!!"

The clerk couldn't think of anything to say back, so Richard just stared at him for a few seconds until I suggested that maybe we should find some other places to put the posters. The captain calmly agreed and we left the store.

A few days later we were standing outside of Gaines Hall, a chemistry building, and Richard was rubbing snow on his face, getting ready to go in and give his reading in the building's main lecture hall. We had arrived at the last minute so I had no idea what awaited us, though Richard seemed fairly confident.

When we entered the place, it was packed wall to wall, all

three hundred seats, with people standing in the aisles. I was amazed. A hush fell over the crowd and the Captain lumbered to the podium. I stood in an entrance and glanced around the room. Even the conservative and religious Dean of Letters and Sciences who had tried to block my tenure was there. Richard started the reading with his poem "Fuck Me Like Fried Potatoes." Suffice it to say, my dean's face looked a little like Richard's face at B. Dalton's.

The Captain Gives
A Couple More Readings With
Me and Other Locals

It was the fall of 1980 when some writers in the Bozeman community decided to have a poetry reading at Chico Hot Springs, which is about fifty miles from Bozeman (twenty miles from Richard's house). One of the people putting it on called me and asked if I'd participate and, with tremulous voice, asked if I'd invite the Captain to participate too.

Richard seemed willing and ready to plunge into "community activities" so before you can say George Dickel, the Captain, my poet-artist friend Dave Waldman, I and several other practitioners of the cinder-block art of poetry were all reading our stuff to a small but attentive audience at Chico Hot Springs. Richard read his poem that goes something like this: "Two guys get out of a car./They stand beside it./They don't know what else to do," and the place erupted. Then I read a poem about trash fish that starts "Here's to the carp, fat on mud bloat and algae," and the place erupted. In fact, probably because of the Captain's presence, people would have erupted if the cook had walked out of the kitchen and farted.

In the fall of '81, the same folks put on the same deal at Chico, but they put Richard on the poster without his permission. He went ape-shit and blamed me, so I contacted the organizers and asked them to print some kind of retraction in the newspaper and one of them called me a spineless sack of pus. At the Captainless reading, I read a poem about bluegrass instruments, including the dobro, and someone sought out Dobro Dick and told him that I had written a sarcastic poem about him. The person didn't know that the dobro itself is a sarcastic instrument, so the whole episode made me feel like hammered chicken shit.

The next year, Richard read with us locals at Chico, but it still wasn't exactly peachy. He got mad at me when I sat next to Paul Ferlazzo, my department head, instead of him and said, "I guess you know which side your bread's buttered on." When he read, of course, the place erupted. No matter what mood he was in, audiences always seemed to come out of the woodwork, ready to erupt for him—as well they should have. I'd just been to England that summer, so I read a poem about a British trash fish called a tench, after which there was a polite scattering of applause. Richard leaned over to me and said, (and I'll always remember this) "That was pretty pre-tench-ous. You need a muse injection, big boy."

Phoney Bologna

With Richard, the phone could be an insidious instrument of torture, a magic portal into the future or both. His voice on his answering machine was straight-forward except for some slight changes and sardonic inflections, a little like his poetry. It went something like this:

"Hello,
as you can probably tell,
I'm not here right now,
but you can leave a message
for when I AM here
after the beep."

Just by his tone I could tell how amused he was to be a voice in the present saying that the source of the voice wasn't present. And somehow he managed to make the word beep sound like a little joke between himself and the listener.

When I first knew him, I was always happy to hear his voice
when he called. I liked to play the fool to his tricky diction.

"Hello."

"Hello, it's me."

"Hello, me."

"What's the big boy up to today?"

"No good."

"Sounds interesting. Perhaps you can come over the hill and
we can do some damage."

"Sure."

"Shurrr—you Oklahomans certainly gave a way with words.
On your way, how about stopping and picking up a little Dickel.

"Black or white?"

"The sun is out and it's June, so white. I'll pay you back."

"Uh huh."

"Do I detect an element doubt in your voice?"

"Huh uh. I'll be over in an hour or so."

"I'll have the ice cubes ready."

As time wore on—through a considerable pile of both black
and white label Dickel bottles, I got so I wasn't quite so excited
about Richard and his magic telephone. Frequently when I needed
to get in touch with him about plans we'd left vague earlier, I'd
call and his phone would be unplugged, and this would lead to
odd bouts of recrimination when he'd call me wondering why I

hadn't called. Even more disarming were his three a.m. calls, frequently from other countries. Sometimes they were important— as when we were arranging for his quarter residency here at M.S.U. Other times, he might just be depressed and needing someone to talk to. Either way, they were dream calls where I'd just been dredged up out of r.e.m. sleep. Looking back, the calls still seem like dreams. In fact, since then I've dreamed calls from Richard, and in the morning, in those few minutes between waking and sleeping, I've wondered if they were real. Here's a blend of a real call and a dream call—collect.

Ring, ring, ring, ring, ring, ring, ring, ring.

"Hello."

"Will you accept a collect call from Richard Brautigan?"

"Wha, uh."

"Will you accept a collect call from Richard Brautigan?"

"Uh, Yes."

"Hello there big boy. Sounds like I woke you up."

"Sort of."

"So you still must be sort of asleep."

"No, now I'm sort of awake."

"It's dreary here. It's been dreary for a long time."

"In Tokyo?"

"No, in Amsterdam. "

"Are you o.k.?"

"It's dreary here."

"So you aren't o.k.?"

"Dreary–for a long time."

"Do I hear the jingling of ice cubes?"

"Yes, they are very expensive ice cubes."

"Well, they jingle nicely."

"They should. Have you been fishing this winter?"

"Yes, ice fishing–for perch."

"Are you still catching them by using their eyes for bait?"

"Of course."

"Explain how you do that again."

"I catch a perch, I stun it on the ice, I pop out an eye, I put it on the hook, and I catch another perch, I stun it on the ice, I pop out an eye..."

"An eye for an eye."

"Yes."

"If they could talk, they would probably say, 'I'll keep an eye out for you.'"

"Probably."

"You sound tired. You should probably go back to bed."

"Probably."

"I'll call you when it's less dreary."

"O.k."

"Bye, big guy."

"Bye, Richard, hang in there."

"Ah yes, hang–dreary."

"I only meant...."

Click.

Here's a letter I got a couple of weeks after whatever part of that call was real.

Amsterdam, January 19, 1984

Dear Greg,

I'm sorry I woke you up at the beginning of this month, but what else could I do? It was impossible to resist.

Love
Richard

PS Send the bill to Joe, so he can put it on the stack.

(Joe Swindlehurst was Richard's lawyer in Livingston.)

We All Look Alike

Richard and I were both tall blond and pink. Actually, I was sort of a mottled pink because I liked to lie in the sun and damage my skin–at least until skin cancer set in about ten years after his death. Richard avoided the sun like a vampire. In any case, I think that, to the Japanese who saw us, we may have been a big, hulking American stereotype.

I know that when those four Japanese journalists from FM Tokyo and Pioneer Stereo came to interview Richard for the *Welcome to Hard Times* segment on Montana writers, they did sort of a double take after they saw us standing together there in his front yard. In spite of the fact that they were all named Ken, they didn't look much alike. Ken Okubo looked like an intellectual. Ken Nagano, looked like a Hollywood mover and shaker, and Kaneo (I can't remember his last name), looked like a techno-geek. Oddly enough, they did what they looked like. Actually, there was a fourth who wasn't named Ken, but I can't remember what he did.

We all spent a memorable June afternoon wandering around Richard's place while he struck noble poses and made sweeping majestic statements about the West. Kaneo followed him, holding up a microphone attached to a tiny miraculous device (miraculous for the early '80s) that made studio-quality recordings. After a while, Richard asked them to record me pretending to arrive at his place then performing one of my songs, so I played "The Ballad of Billy Montana."

Later, Ken Nagano said, with the ease and flair of a Hollywood mover and shaker, that there was great demand for songwriters and musicians.

During a break in the recording, Richard took me aside and taught me a brief Japanese phrase to repeat for his guests. To the present day, I've never known what it meant, but when I said it, they all started bowing. After they recorded the Captain shooting cans with his .22 pump action rifle for a while, he suggested that we go for a ride up to the top of Trail Creek, so we all piled in my Mazda and headed out.

I was a little nervous because Richard had brought a bottle of Jack Daniels and kept passing it among them. I think he had somehow convinced them that if they declined they were violating a native tradition.

At any rate, by the time we pulled over at the pass, they were all pale and trembling. I thought it must have been the whisky, but Richard later explained that there were no dirt roads in their part of Japan and the washboard ride up the mountain had scared the bajeezus out of them.

Back at El Rancho Brautigan, Richard fixed us all pepper steaks, but they just nibbled the edges of theirs. Richard told me that they would probably put in for combat pay when they returned to Tokyo.

A couple of years later, another Japanese crew from Pioneer Stereo came to the area to make commercials. Since Richard was away, they seemed to be grasping at straws, so they came to my house in Bozeman to interview me about how I thought their products might function in the Montana wilderness. I, of course, had no idea, but with a little help from Judy, I came up with a jingle for them:

My pickup's stalled, my barn burned down.
My wife left with the horse.
My kids are in San Francisco
And are hippies now, of course.
My neighbor took my whisky
And drank up my last beer,
But I've still got my stereo,
And it's a Pioneer.

When they seemed tickled with the song and said they'd pass it along to their boss, Mr. Kato, I felt a little like Richard's Bozeman body double, the way they bustled around me with their equipment. Before they left, they invited me to come to their motel to be "compensated" for my efforts, so I popped in on them the next day and was a bit surprised to see Japanese nudie magazines strewn about the room. "Here, take one home with you," said an efficient looking young man in black horn-rimmed glasses with $150 in one hand and a nudie magazine in the other.

I declined the magazine and probably should have declined the cash, for, as I left, I somehow felt that I'd tarnished the image of big blond American doofuses everywhere. When Richard returned and I told him what I'd done, he did little to discourage this notion.

"They gave you money?"

"Well, uh, yes—but just a hundred dollars or so."

"Or so?"

"Well, maybe a hundred and fifty."

"Maybe?"

The way the Captain was grilling me, and by the tone he was taking, I felt the conversation might just as well have gone something like this:

"They gave you silver?"

"Well, uh, yes—but just twenty-five pieces or so.

"Or so?"

"Well, maybe thirty."

Another company to contact me was Japanese Jim Beam. Richard was in the area and they had tried to get ahold of him, but he had been illusive, so they called me and asked if I'd talk to him. I stupidly agreed and called him.

"Ah, so now you are my Japanese agent?"

"Well, no, I just...."

"You just were hoping to get your hands on a little money?"

"No, I only...."

"Did you know that they want to use me and my house to make a whisky commercial?"

"They didn't tell...."

"Did you know they would pay me a lot of money to make this commercial?"

"I had no...."

"But since you have decided to be my agent, here is what I want you to tell them."

"Yes?"

"I want you to tell them to get fucked."

"I don't think...."

"That's right. You don't think. You just tell them to get fucked." Click.

I knew the Captain had been drinking more lately, but I didn't realize that he would turn his vitriol on the Japanese as well as his friends. The next time the Jim Beam guy called, I told him that Richard wasn't feeling well and that he didn't want to involve himself in any projects for quite a while. The man became distraught and started speaking in a strange poetic voice saying something about a blue window, or a cold blue wind. I told him I was sorry but there was nothing I could do. The next time I talked to Richard, he told me that the guy was hinting at suicide. I thought that was awful, but Richard only said, "It is his decision."

A few months later the Captain reconsidered and accused me of losing him a huge contract and a lot of money. I said, "I'm no agent," and he said, "No shit!"

In a less traumatic way, Japanese women also seemed to confuse me with Richard. Masako kept in touch with me, even after Richard's death, but another more recent and perhaps more contorted episode springs to mind. After his triumphant "Fuck Me Like Fried Potatoes" reading at the M.S.U. Chemistry building, a young Japanese woman from one of my Freshman writing classes came blushing and bowing to the podium to meet him and have him sign her copy of *Sombrero Fall-Out*. When he finished, she trotted out as fast as her little feet could carry her, and I thought he was going to trip trying to catch up with her, but she vanished, having no idea that her idol was in hot lumbering pursuit.

In subsequent writing classes, she would hardly ever look at me and she blushed when she did. Shortly after the quarter was over, I saw her again through the front window of my living room where I was wandering around in my underwear. I was reading some poetry and glanced up just in time to see her passing in a car. I didn't think she could see me, but just as I recognized her, I saw that she was looking at my front window so intensely that she bumped into the car in front of her. I went to my room to put on some clothes, and when I came back she was nowhere to be seen.

Richard loved this story and had me repeat it to him several times. Later, the whole thing culminated in her marrying a big blond Bozeman Police officer who lived across the street from me. She had obviously found an available one of us and married it.

Right Up to My Ears

We had just finished rearranging the Harry Dean Stanton coffee table (the rotted side of an old wooden wagon box that Harry Dean Stanton had seen in the creek near Richard's house and had made the mistake of saying it would make a good antique, so the Captain dredged it up, put a shiny brass label on it saying The Harry Dean Stanton Coffee Table and propped it in his front yard) and were sitting on the hood of a 1956 Ford Victoria (which two "boys from Texas" had abandoned to rot between his house and barn), examining the stars when Richard said, "I hope some young English professor will write a book about my work some day."

I leaned back on the hood of the Ford Victoria, which was still warm even though the sun had set almost an hour before, looked up at a particularly thick clump of stars, and said, "Me too."

To Richard, writing was like mining gold from the air or, yes, "loading mercury with a pitch fork." Whether the ink was from the tip of his pen or from the ribbon of his typewriter, it came slowly, deliberately and miraculously, as if he couldn't get over the fact that he could make letters, words and sentences out of practically nothing except what was in his head. For him, even writing a check was like some arduous process where his squiggly little signature was squeezed out through a deeply mysterious alchemy. And he would clean his typewriter and replace its ribbon as if it were a delicate tool which facilitated the flow of information between parallel universes.

That's not to say he wasn't practical about it. Once over smoked whitefish in my T.V. room, he told me that if it weren't for his excellent high school English teacher, he never would have known how important grammar and punctuation are. He said he still had his high school writing text book and he always wrote with a copy of *Strunk and White's Elements of Style* beside him.

He spoke in horror of a time when a small press published an expensive hand-made book of his poetry and left an "it's" where an "its" should have been.

When I knew him, Richard trusted some of his friends more than he trusted professional agents and editors when it came to revising his manuscripts. He made some major textual changes and even changed the title of his posthumous novel, *An Unfortunate Woman,* after Becky Fonda read it and made appropriate suggestions. I'm glad he let her have her way; otherwise, the novel might have been called "Investigating Moods." To express his gratefulness to

Becky and Marian for their help on So the Wind Won't Blow It All Away, he dedicated the novel to them under their maiden names.

To me, Richard's work is defenseless. I told him this shortly after we met and he looked at me over his spectacles as if he were examining a dead bug. I didn't want him to get the wrong idea, so I proceeded to compare his work to a big bunny. The bunny just sits or hops around as bunnies do, but it is a perfect bunny. It doesn't try to be a tiger or a kangaroo or a swan because it knows what it is: a bunny–not just a bunny, but especially a bunny.

Sometimes a critic will come along and say something like, "Hey, this is just a bunny!" or "What the hell is a bunny doing HERE!" or "What the fuck kind of cutting horse is THIS!" and give the bunny a good, hard kick. The interesting thing is that the bunny doesn't change because of this. It just goes right on hopping miraculously across the page, reinventing its bunniness every step of the way.

After I said something like this, Richard removed his spectacles and suggested that it might be a good time for a drink, during which he told me that one reader had been so offended by *The Pill Versus the Spring Hill Mining Disaster* that he mailed it to the Captain with a turd squashed in it. "How," asked Richard, "does that fit into your bunny comparison?"

Back then, when I'd travel to professional conferences like the Modern Language Association, I'd bring up the Captain's work just to test the waters. Responses ranged from huffy dismissals to incensed rants. I think, to a certain extent, Richard depended on this reaction because, without it, his parody would have existed in a vacuum.

In the days of Minimalism, Feminism, Post-Formalism, Post-Modernism, Post-Humanism, Post-Structuralism, Post-Etc., scholars don't seem nearly so put off by his work; however, even while he was alive, Mark Chenier, the French Deconstructionist critic, saw his work worthy of a lengthy, esoteric discourse, (to which Richard responded, "The Frog's got it right.")

I'd attribute this reevaluation to a tendency toward calling everything into question, especially the dwems (dead white European males) of the literary canon, where, to be good, in T.S. Eliot's words, an "individual talent" has to have his (and I do mean HIS) roots in the "tradition" of Western Civilization. Though Richard knew a hell of a lot about this tradition, he also loathed any tendency of a writer to parade his knowledge of it before the reader. And, though fiction is necessarily based on pretending, he hated pretentiousness. You can see this in his prose. Whenever he catches himself being overtly symbolic or profound, the language turns back and beats itself over the head. Or, as he says in his poem, "Taking No Chances," in *June 30th, June 30th:*

I am that which begins
but has no beginning.
I am also full of shit
right up to my ears.

Because it's out of print and, to
me, one of Richard's more defenseless
(therefore more representative)
novels, I'll use some examples from
Willard and His Bowling Trophies.

Richard loved Hemingway's life
and works and took up his model's
brief, stoic declarative sentences with
no qualms. But as soon as that
cadence started establishing a macho

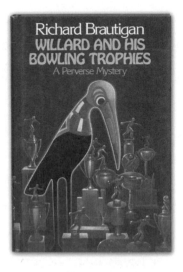

tone, Richard made sure the "grace under pressure" turned clumsy
and inept. In the following, the Captain takes on Henry Miller's
sexual taboos and Hemingway's masculine prowess with Bob, a
man who feels compelled to gently bind and gag his wife,
Constance, because he has warts up the end of his penis and can't
have normal sex. (Bob got the warts from Constance who got
them from a one night stand with a lawyer during a bout of
depression when her well-reviewed novel sold poorly.)

About once in every ten times he would gag her effectively.

He just didn't have it together any more. He knew that his failures annoyed her, but what else could he do?

His whole life was a sloppy painful mess.

He had used adhesive tape for a while. The tape always gagged her effectively but she didn't like the way it hurt when he pulled it off. Even if he pulled it off very gently, it still hurt like hell so the tape had to go.

So much for noble language. So much for manly, assertive sentences. So much for alluring perversity. So much for grace under pressure. So much for the formalist edict that the author remain separate from the work since the author himself had herpes, was concerned about book sales and was into bondage. No wonder the neo-feminists let this big bunny go limping away. No wonder the minimalists glom onto him like frayed adhesive tape. Every word here says "I surrender."

A few pages later, Bob reads Constance two fragments from *The Greek Anthology* while she lies before him, carefully and considerately (though clumsily) bound and gagged.

"Here are two really beautiful ones," Bob said. "'Deeply do I mourn, for my friends are nothing worth.' 'Takes bites of the cucumbers.'"

"What do you think? Do you like them?" Bob said.
He had forgotten that there was a gag in her mouth.

So much for Classicism. So much for Romanticism. So much for tradition. So much for the individual talent. So much for Western Civilization.

I sometimes think Richard would write books and, for that matter, hold conversations, just so he could repeat words that he liked, and these words were usually strategically placed to parody pomposity. Once he got on a favorite word, he would return to it much like he would return to his door to make sure it was locked.

The Captain always liked the word beer, and, when we were at a bar, he delighted in talking about the beer I was drinking, especially if it was in a can.

"Like that can of beer, big boy?

"Sure do."

"You certainly seem to have command of that beer can. How much beer do you have left in that can?"

"Not much."

"I think we'd better get the big boy another can of beer. I'd certainly hate to see that commanding beer grip without a can of beer in it."

In *Willard and His Bowling Trophies,* Richard describes one of the Logan brothers (three guys who are pursuing their stolen bowling trophies) totally in terms of his beer drinking.

The beer drinking Logan brother had finished his beer. It was his last one and he wished that he had another one. He had become quite a beer drinker since the bowling trophies had been stolen. He wanted to go out for another beer but he didn't say anything about it. His brothers did not approve of him drinking beer all the time and he had been lucky to have the beer that he had just finished.

I could try to come up with a profound reason why Richard liked to say and write the word beer, but I'd really rather go find me a can of beer.

I think he wrote *Willard and His Bowling Trophies* so he could repeat those title words over and over. The combination is so dead-pan, so anti-Romantic.

Willard and the bowling trophies were in the front room of a big apartment. It was night and dark in the front room but even so there was a faint religious glow coming from the bowling trophies.

Saint Willard of the Stolen Bowling Trophies!

So much for the sacred and the profane.

Richard also liked to use the word bowling in conversation whenever the opportunity presented itself–and sometimes when it didn't. Once I took him fishing on the East Gallatin River near Bozeman and he dubbed it The Little Bowling Ball because it seems so proletarian with its smell of creosote and its riprap of old car bodies and probably because it's such a shabby (but trout-rich) excuse for a river among the mythic blue-ribbon streams of Montana.

As we tried to drift our flies through sunken car windows, Richard went on and on about underwater bowling, bowling for trophy trout, bowling ball baptisms, etc., until, in his usual non-sequitur way, he spotted an abandoned log cabin across a field and clomped toward it shrieking, "Tara! I'll never go hungry again!"

Deflation and parody seemed to be in Richard's blood. He took on many of the Great American Novel's serious genres by turning quests and conflicts into absurd dilemmas. In *Dreaming of Babylon,* an archetypal gum-shoe detective spends most of his time trying to find bullets for his pistol. In *The Hawkline Monster,* two cowboys ride out of their Western and find themselves in a Gothic romance, replete with a basement full of chemicals and a couple of sinister sisters itching for a fuckfest. *So the Wind Won't Blow It All Away,* a rendition of the great American Tragedy, sends the young protagonist to buy ammo for his .22 rifle rather than a hamburger, resulting in the death of his best friend and digressions on hamburgers that bear comparison to the discourse on whales and cetology in *Moby Dick*.

Jesus, I'm starting to use words like replete, rendition, protagonist and discourse, and I haven't even arrived at his poetry yet. Before you know it, I'll be using words like indeed and foregrounding. I think I'll quit while the quittin's good.

Goodbye Bolinas

hen Judy, Chris, Max and I visited Bolinas in early August
of 1984, Richard wasn't prepared for the whole family.
When he called, I had just indicated that I was coming, but our
car was broken down and in a shop in San Francisco, and Judy
and the kids didn't want to sit around my brother's house and
wait, so I drove my brother's car, and they came with me.
As the Captain came down the hill to meet me, his mouth
literally dropped open. But he adjusted quickly and we went
up to his house.

Though it was a wonderful old redwood place sitting up on
a hill, disguised by trees and blackberry bushes, the interior was
depressing as hell. Richard had shut off all but two or three rooms
for living. In the barren fireplace were a few shreds of burned
newspapers. Next to that, the usual unmade bed, a ripped-up
naugahyde sofa, a table full of letters asking publishers to please
pay him, and a cardboard box full of wadded-up twenty dollar
bills. The Captain said to Judy, "Now I'm going to show you some

California hospitality." Eventually, that meant that we were going to eat Dutch treat cantaloupe and tuna fish sandwiches on the deck. Judy and Richard both ruffled at each other a little but got along pretty well considering. Richard asked Chris and Max if they were Trekies. They said they were, so he sat them down in front of a dismal little black and white TV to watch "Star Trek." Recently Max told me he even had a brief conversation with Richard which went as follows:

Richard: What grade are you in?

Max: Sixth.

Richard: That's a shitty grade.

Earlier, he had been keeping very close tabs on the Olympics. He was really in the USA spirit and even said "USA USA" a few times. Richard was always proud to be an American. On his back porch in Montana, sometimes he would look off over the mountains and say (in Imperial Mode) we are Americans. We are THE Americans. He gave us a little talk on how good television was getting and seriously discussed what improvements shows like "Remington Steel," "The A Team," and "Scarecrow and Mrs. King" were. He said he had quite a few projects going and that he was optimistic about several things that he was awaiting news on, including screenplays and books.

When Judy and the kids went for a walk, he started telling me a little about his childhood which he had seldom discussed before.

He said that he had been the leader of a gang of teenagers that did a lot of damage. He said that if only the school he had attended had cared more about his mind, things might have been different, land they might have saved the county a lot of money. He then said that his main problem with school had been dyslexia. When he had been in Japan that spring, he and some Japanese friends figured it out. I thought a while and figured there must be some truth in it. Whenever I saw him write checks or notes, it was as if he were squeezing gold out of lead. The writing was cramped and wiggly and an obvious effort.

His professional writing is also deceptively simple, though the ideas and style are much more profound than the immediate facade lets on. He said, "Just think of all the money my childhood community would have saved in vandalism and bringing me to justice if they had tried to figure out my problem and done something about it." Then I said, "But maybe if you had been cured we wouldn't have gotten all of your books." And he said, "Or maybe they would have been better." I shook my head. Richard had always been exceptionally intelligent and was always surprising me with what he had read and what he knew about—in detail.

But he was a slow reader; thus, all of that knowledge must have come at a high cost of time and concentration. Richard once told me that he never finished high school, but Tom McGuane told me that before he shot himself, he propped up his high school diploma, his reading glasses and a copy of *All Watched Over by Machines of Loving Grace* next to him.

After Judy and the kids returned, we sent the boys off exploring, and the Captain took us on a walking tour of Bolinas. He kept saying, "Look how beautiful it is." And it was: long stone paths going down hills of gardens and trees, panoramic vistas of the coastline, seagulls whirling and shrieking. As all of this went on around us, Richard said, "I'm happy." I said, "Let me get a tape recorder." And he went back to Imperial Mode. But I think he actually was happy.

I think maybe he had made a decision, though, because he kept confusing his future plans, at one time acting like he was going to stay in Bolinas, at another, asking me to start the wheels rolling on another teaching stint at Montana State. He gave me pictures and tokens to take back to his other friends in Bozeman: one pewter corn cob holder for Brad, a booth snapshot of himself for Scoop and Schrieber, a request to call for Sean. Looking back, I guess maybe he was saying goodbye.

Later that evening, we bought Dutch treat pizza. He asked the boys what kind they wanted, and they said, "anything but anchovy," so he ordered two anchovy pizzas from a guy who made them in his house down the hill. We took them over to Bob's (the guy whose boat didn't work) in Stinson Beach. He and his wife were obviously preoccupied with the Olympics and a new baby, but we made polite conversation, ate the pizza and watched the sun set on the Pacific.

Of course, it took us an hour to find the house in the hills above Stinson Beach, so we spent the usual amount of time in confused driving. I sometimes called Richard the Pershing II because it was so damned hard for him to get off the pad. Finding Bob's house was no different. Anyway, when it got to be about 10:30, we asked Richard if we could take him home because we had to drive all the way back to Berkeley on Sir Francis Drake Blvd. Richard was glassy-eyed and fading by then. "Don't worry," he said. "You know me. I'll always find a way home." And that was the last I ever saw of him.

Captain Random

If I try to recall Richard in specific ways, the memory usually breaks down. If I think of his obsession with Japanese women and culture, I'm distracted by how he and Aki would follow his favorite high school girls' basketball team around the small towns of Montana. If I think of him as a confirmed, dyed-in-the-wool alcoholic, I remember how his skin started to turn orange shortly before his last departure when he was living on a diet of carrots and water. Though a blizzard kept me from attending his goodbye party at the Fondas, I heard tales of him and Tom McGuane, the original carousers, hanging around the Perrier and vegetables all evening.

If I think of him as secure, famous and confident, tossing off such phrases as, "I've made my mark," or "The cat's in the bag and the bag's in the river," a mess of opposing images comes crowding in, images such as that of Richard the Pershing II. We named him after that missle which often came crashing back into the pad soon after it took off. In more familiar terms, leaving his house with him was a bit like trying to accompany a yo-yo. Before we got out the door he'd check several times to make sure that the lights, stove, etc., were turned off. Once we were out the door, he'd lock it, turn the handle to make sure it was locked, turn around to leave, turn back around to make sure it was locked, turn around and walk toward the car, turn around and walk back to make sure the door was locked, turn around, walk to the car, get in, get back out, walk back to the door, make sure it was locked, turn around, walk to the car, get in, etc. Sometimes we'd even get a few hundred yards down the road and he'd still want to return to check the BACK door.

Richard's suicide was about as random and contradictory as his other behavior. He had always insisted that he would never take his own life. He even told little stories about people whose suicide attempts had been foiled. In one of these episodes, a man had walked in to find a woman friend with her head in her oven and the gas on. In the Captain's rendition, the man quietly left, went around behind the house, and turned off the main gas supply.

So when, one gloomy afternoon in the early fall, Brad Donovan summoned me to the Owl Bar in Livingston to talk about Richard, I saw it as a welcome break in my routine. Though I'd just visited him in Bolinas the month before, he hadn't been to Montana in over a year, so I was hoping that Brad had news of his immanent return. Besides, I'd always enjoyed the Owl.

Richard once had a pipe dream of buying the place, setting up a cot in the back and subsisting on intravenous whisky.

Once I got settled behind my standard Owl fare, tomato juice and draft beer, Brad broke the news that Richard had "bought the farm." I thought, oh great, that's all he needs, a farm. When will the big oaf learn. Hell, he already has a little ranch, and he's piled up some whopping debts in Tokyo staying at the ritziest hotel.

"What farm?" I said.

"You know," said Brad. "He's BOUGHT THE FARM."

I was still trying to figure out which farm he'd bought and why he'd bought it. Maybe he'd bought a farm above his property to avoid disputes over water, maybe....

"He shot himself," said Brad. "He killed himself."

A Happy Day

Tokyo, May 12, 1983

Dear Greggie,
Well, here we are: meeting on a piece of paper that has
traveled across the Pacific Ocean to reach the hands
fish dread in Montana. It is a quiet morning here in Tokyo.
I had some ham and eggs for breakfast, coffee. This
afternoon I'll go to a little cafe and do some writing.

Maybe I'll watch some TV tonight.

...and then yawn and yawn and yawn again and then
  Z Z Z

Love,
Richard

About the Author

Greg Keeler has taught English at Montana State University since 1975.
He's published seven books of poetry, the most recent being *The Sea
Widow's Journal: To a Fisherman Drowned* (Tapir Press, 2000). Known for
his satiric and flat-out funny poems and songs, he's recorded 14 CDs and
tapes, his latest being *Subliminable.* He's written music for several plays
and musicals, and he reads and performs often for many benefits and good
causes. Having received several awards for his teaching and writing,
he was awarded the Governor's Award in the Humanities in 2001
by the Montana Committee for the Humanities.

9/09   2   12/04